> *"We make sense of the world through mental models, not just accumulating facts. Mental models help us recognize patterns. A good model allows us to see different things every time we look at it! The best mental models are simple, flexible, and open enough to capture complex situations and encourage us to see more, and ask better questions."*

- Marc Applebaum, PhD

ScrumZone.org is an organization focused on Organizational Scrum: Single-team and Multi-Team

Book Design by Tuna Traffic, LLC

First Edition publication date: December 25, 2017

ISBN-10: 1981222995
ISBN-13: 978-1981222995

SCRUM HANDBOOK

SINGLE-TEAM SCRUM

Dan Rawsthorne
Chief Scientist
3Back, LLC

Doug Shimp
President
3Back, LLC

What is Scrum?

Single-Team Scrum Description

Scrum Glossary

Table of Contents

SECTION I

What is Scrum?

Scrum is Scrum, and it's a beautiful thing. Unfortunately, Scrum has been described in many different, inconsistent, and incoherent ways. By focusing solely on Product Ownership we arrive at three common, existing, and different, descriptions of Scrum – which we refer to as $Scrum_P$, $Scrum_G$ and $Scrum_H$.

We both fell in love with Scrum in the late 1990's. It was clean, elegant, agile, and echoed all the good Teams we'd seen in our lives: in sports, in the military, and on the construction site. At its core, Scrum simply says:

- Have a Team that gets its work done all by itself, and is not at the mercy of others;
- Have a Product Owner that is the single-source of requirements for the Team, so there is no bickering or arguing about what to do;
- Have a Scrum Master to help improve process and remove Impediments; and
- Have multiple, frequent, feedback loops in order to be appropriately agile.

What a beautiful concept!

Since then we have seen, and helped, many teams implement Scrum. We have seen that Scrum can be successfully implemented by a Team if it has the freedom and authority to do so. Of course, each implementation is different in the details, as it adapts to its own environment and situation – but the core of Scrum will be there, and the Team will succeed.

Enlightened Organizations see that Scrum works, and they want some. These Organizations can see how powerful good Teams led by a single Product Owner can be. The problem is, they want to know how to make Scrum work for them — they want to know how to build their own Scrum Teams — so at their core they want definitions, recipes, or instructions...

Because of this need, we (the Scrum Community) had to develop Frameworks, Guidance, and Rules about Scrum. We had to be able to describe how to *tailor* Scrum to the Organizations where it lives. We had to be able to tell stories about how Scrum can be used to help Organizations provide value.

Originally, these stories were based on the experiences of us storytellers, and described how we had seen Scrum work. These stories had to be targeted at the Organizations we were trying to help, as they were useful only to the extent that they helped the Organizations provide value.

And we found that Product Ownership, in particular, was very difficult to describe in a consistent way. The concept of Product Ownership was clear — be a single-source of requirements for the Team — but the implementation was not. Organizations have different needs, and we saw three different versions of the Product Ownership story emerge.

These versions of Product Ownership lead to different variants (or strains) of Scrum, which we refer to as *Scrum*$_P$, Scrum$_G$, and Scrum$_H$. Each of them was created because of different "forces" in the Organization. We will give a brief overview of each, but first let me tell you a *simple* story about Scrum... what most people would accept as a solid, high-level, description of Scrum.

Basic Scrum Description

Scrum is an agile, team-based, model of production that describes how a single **Team** produces valuable **Results** (often called **Product**) for **Stakeholders** in a complex development environment. While the behaviors described in the Scrum model have been around for decades – if not centuries – the first documented description of Scrum for software was presented at OOPSLA 1995, by Ken Schwaber.

At its core, Scrum is very simple, with few rules and definitions. Here is a typical description.

First,

Scrum has only four Roles:

1. **Stakeholders** are people who want the Results;

2. The **Team** is a self-organizing, cross-functional, group that produces the Results for the Stakeholders;

3. The **Product Owner** does Product Ownership; working with both the Stakeholders and the Team to assure that the 'right' Results are being produced in the 'right' order; and

4. The **Scrum Master** does Scrum Mastering; improving the ability for the Team to do its work.

Second,

There are two cadences in Scrum, punctuated by 'Inspect and Adapt' events that enable Scrum to be agile:

1. The Team has a **Daily Scrum** (typically 15 minutes long or less) to discuss what was worked on since the last Daily Scrum, and create a 'plan' for what will be worked on until the next Daily Scrum *(the Daily Scrum works well with our natural, circadian, rhythm and is typically used to start the work day);* and

2. The Team has a **Sprint** (typically 1-4 weeks long) to accomplish progress towards work goals; at the end of which the Team has 1) a **Review**, with the Product Owner and Stakeholders, of the Results it produced; 2) a **Retrospective**, which is an internal conversation about improving *how* the Team does its work; and 3) a **Planning** session with the Product Owner to determine what Results should be produced during the next Sprint. *(The Sprint cadence works well with the Stakeholder and Organization rhythms, interrupting them often enough to get meaningful feedback for the Team, but not so often that they feel 'put upon'.)*

Third,

There are three artifacts in Scrum *(note: remember that the Team's Results have historically been called Product)*:

1. The **Product Increment**, which is the result of the work the Team has done, and is the current version of the Team's Results;

2. The **Product Backlog**, which is a list of new, or additional, Results that the Stakeholders want, and the order in which they will be worked on; and

3. The **Sprint Backlog**, which contains a list of Tasks that the Team is working on in the current Sprint.

Most people would agree that this is a good description of Scrum. Within this description, however, there is a lot of ambiguity, and this ambiguity has caused many strains of Scrum to emerge – often because of differences in **Product Ownership**, which we define as *"the collection of Responsibilities and Accountabilities that sit between the Stakeholders and the Developers."* Basically, Product Ownership is what converts the 'wants and needs' of Stakeholders into work for Dev Teams. In practice, we have seen three basic kinds of Product Ownership, which we refer to as *Scrum*$_P$, Scrum$_G$, and Scrum$_H$, as you see in the figure to the right.

In the next few sections, we will give more detailed explanations of these three strains of Scrum.

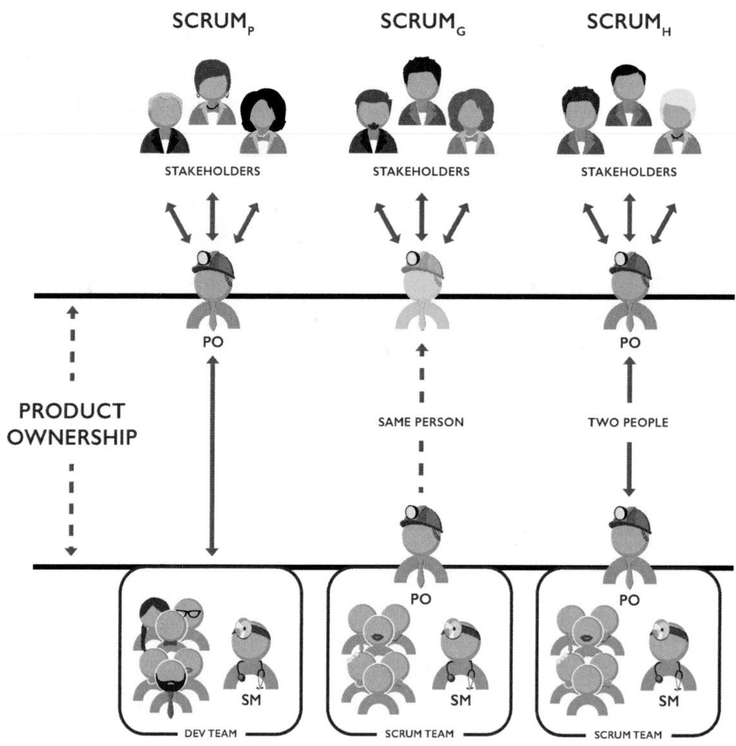

Figure 1:Three Strains of Product Ownership

Scrum$_P$ Overview

Early implementations of Scrum enabled a single Team to develop a single Product for a single set of (relatively cohesive) Stakeholders. To do this, there was a Product Owner *outside* the Team with the Stakeholders. This Product Owner prioritizes requirements, at the beginning of a Sprint, at a fairly high level, and works with the DevTeam to develop a Sprint Backlog that describes how they will implement these requirements. The DevTeam commits to the requirements, the Sprint Backlog is 'locked down', and the DevTeam is left alone to develop. Even though the Product Owner can't 'mess with' the Team during the Sprint, the Team can work with the Product Owner during the Sprint in order to get a better understanding of the requirements.

As intended, this type of Scrum works well for developing a single Product for a single set of Stakeholders, especially if the requirements are emergent and not overly volatile. This type of Scrum is still around, still being useful.

We refer to this type of Scrum as *Scrum$_P$*, and one of its popular variants is described in the *Scrum Primer*, found at www.scrumprimer.org.

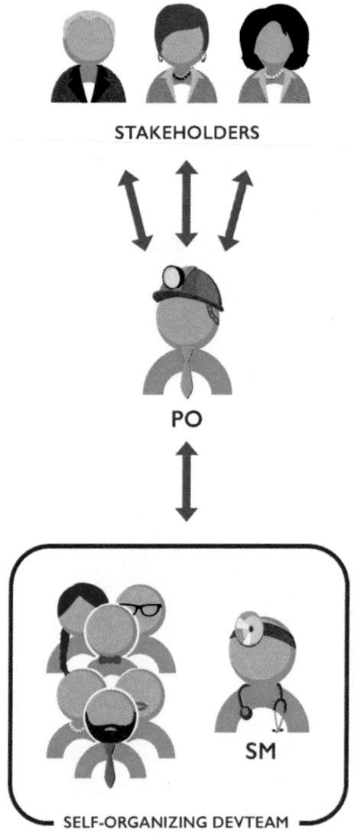

Figure 2: Scrum$_P$ Structure

Scrum$_G$ Overview

However, there is often the need for this single Team to not only *develop* the Product, but *maintain* the Product once it has been deployed. This requires the Team to be interrupted frequently in order to resolve time-sensitive issues related to bugs, building, testing or deployment that come up in Operations. The Team needs to know: *"Which is more important, the new functionality we're already working on, or the new work that just came up?"* and this is a decision the Product Owner needs to make *right now*; the Product Owner needs to be agile all the time.

A 'Business Side' Product Owner (as we see in *Scrum$_P$*) is often incapable of making these decisions in a timely manner, and the response to this problem was to move the Product Owner onto the Team in order to be available to the Team to prioritize these interrupts real-time. The Product Owner still works with the Stakeholders to gather and prioritize the functional requirements, but lives on the Team in order to prioritize new work as needed. The Sprint Backlog is malleable (changes can be negotiated at any time), and the Team commits to a Sprint Goal rather than the totality of the Sprint Backlog in order to allow the Team some 'wiggle room' concerning what they actually have to build.

As intended, this works well for developing and maintaining a single Product in production, as long as the development requirements are not overly volatile *and* the Product Owner has ready access to the Stakeholders for advice.

We refer to this type of Scrum as Scrum$_G$, and its most popular variant is described in the *Scrum Guide*, found at www.scrumguides.org.

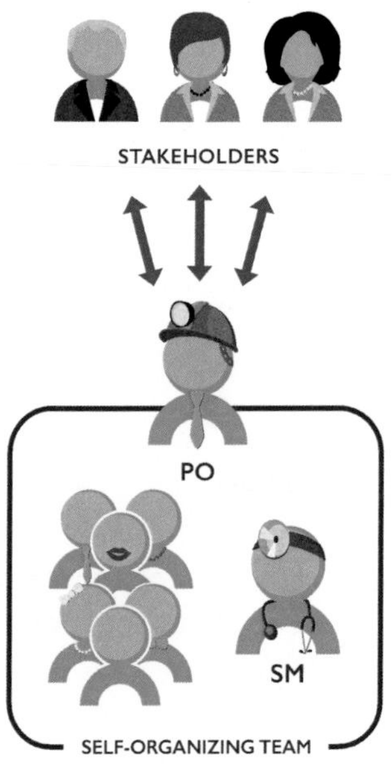

Figure 3: Scrum$_G$ Structure

Scrum$_H$ Overview

As you can see, these first two types of Scrum (P and G) are mutually incompatible (PO inside vs. outside, Sprint Backlog locked-down vs. malleable), but each is useful when used appropriately. They are both simple and easy to understand, and this very simplicity causes problems when people force-fit them into their Organizations. In many cases, neither of these strains of Scrum will work without modifications. Therefore, in order to make Scrum work, many Organizations made modifications, and new variants of Scrum arose.

Many of these variants arose in order to 'fix' problems the Organizations found with Product Ownership. For example, one of the major problems with both of these versions of Scrum is that each of them requires the Product Owner to be an effective link between the major Stakeholders and the Team. The Product Owner must be able to spend a significant amount of time with each group. *(For example, Jeff Sutherland (one of the original authors of Scrum) recommends that the Product Owner spend 'half' his/her time with the Team, and 'half' his/her time with the Stakeholders.)*

So, these Organizations found themselves asking questions like: *"What happens when the Team is developing and maintaining multiple Products, each with its own set of Stakeholders?"* and *"What happens when the Scrum Team is in India, while the Stakeholders are in New York?"* In these cases, and many others, the Team still needs the on-the-team Product Owner for the tactical prioritization of work, but this team-based Product Owner often has trouble managing the necessary Stakeholder interactions and still 'do right' by the Team.

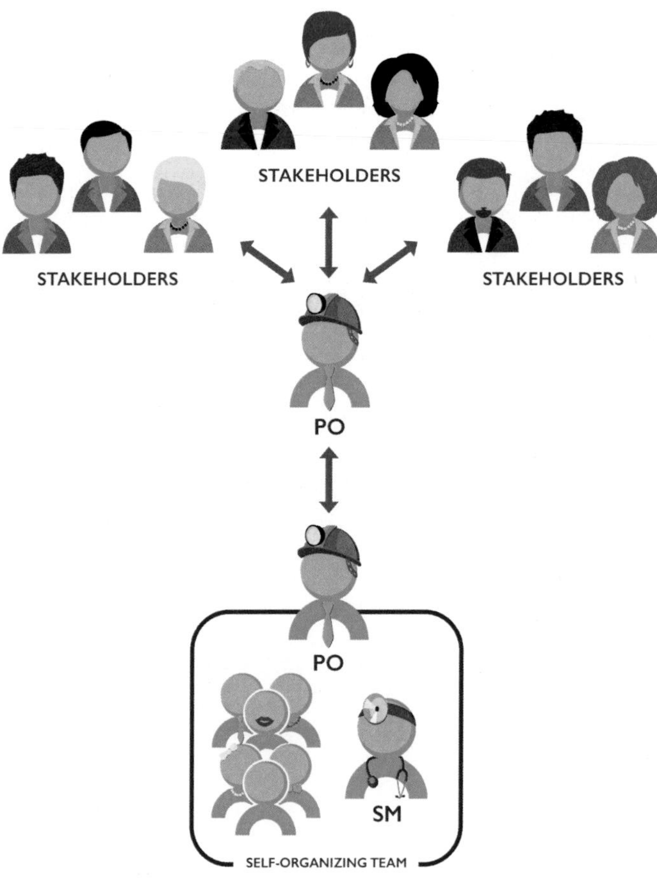

Figure 4: Scrum$_H$ Structure

The result was that another strain of Scrum arose that realizes that there often is a need for two Product Owner-types, one to work with the Stakeholders and prioritize what Products to work on (strategic prioritization), and one with the Scrum Team to prioritize the work being done (tactical prioritization). Since this type of Scrum often occurs when there is more than one Product being produced (from the Organization's perspective), it often doesn't make much sense to call *anybody* a "Product Owner" – there isn't an appropriate, single, Product to own. Therefore we sometimes see names for these roles that more accurately describe their responsibilities (Business Owner, Team Captain, PO Proxy, Chief Product Owner, Squad Leader, Helper PO, and so on).

This is a different kind of Product Ownership... and this kind of Product Ownership is distributed and agile *all the time*. This is a common strain of Scrum in the real-world, and is what many Organizations who try to do Scrum_G end up *actually* doing because a single Product Owner can't do everything that is needed.

We refer to this new version of Scrum as Scrum_H, and it is the subject of this Handbook.

However, Scrum_H goes well beyond simply having two different Product Owner-types. This is the *start* of things – the reason we *need* a new description – but it is not all. There are many other adaptations that are commonly made in order to have a Scrum that is adequate for today's world, and we have combined many of them into Scrum_H. Our goal for Scrum_H is that it helps people understand how Scrum is useful for today's Organizations – Scrum_H does not change Scrum, it just describes it differently – it is a new strain of Scrum, not a new Scrum. The end result is that Scrum_H does several things:

1. $Scrum_H$ defines multiple Stakeholder, Product Ownership, and Scrum Mastering sub-roles (or facets), providing a more realistic model adequate for today's world;

2. $Scrum_H$ extends and unifies both $Scrum_P$ and $Scrum_G$; and

3. $Scrum_H$ is scale-ready; it can respond to growth or be applied to large Organizations without any modifications or additions to the model.

So, let's move on to the $Scrum_H$ model…

SECTION 2

Single-Team Scrum Description

At its core, Scrum is a model showing how a single Team produces Results for Stakeholders. The Scrum_H model of single-Team Scrum is a clean, flexible, description of Scrum that is appropriate for most Organizations...

Teams and Roles

Let's start with a picture. On the left we see the simple view of the Scrum Roles that we find in Scrum_P and Scrum_G. On the right we see how the roles split into the entities we have in Scrum_H. These entities can be thought of as facets of the original roles, or as sub-roles…

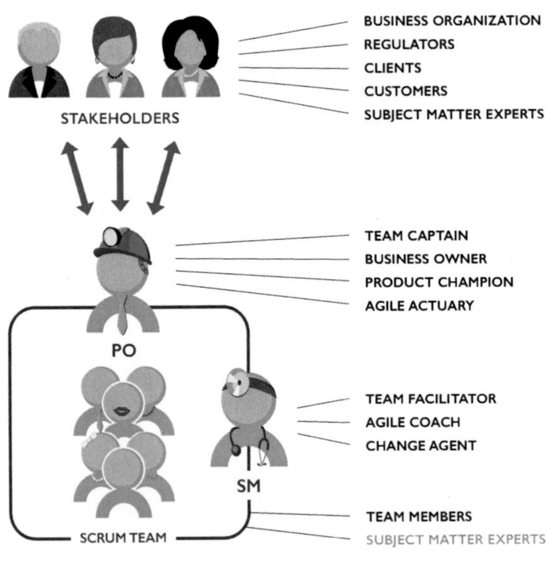

Figure 5: Expanding the Basic Scrum Roles

Now, let's define what we see here…

Stakeholders

A Team does not exist in a vacuum; it is surrounded by **Stakeholders**, who are people who are involved with, affected by, or have an effect on, the Team. There are many kinds of Stakeholders, and some of them *must* be included in our description in order to fully understand Scrum; the Stakeholder Groups we must have names for are:

- The **Business Organization**: The organization the Team belongs to, or works for. The Business Organization provides services the Team needs in order to exist, such as Human Resources, Logistics, Facilities, Contracting, Training, Legal, and so on. The Business Organization is often simply referred to as "the Business" or "the Organization".

- **Regulators**: Entities, either inside or outside your Business Organization, who can regulate, or constrain, the Product/Results the Team is producing and/or the process that the Team uses. Examples include things like Cyber Security, CISA, ITAR Compliance, SOX, Medical, etc.

- **Clients**: The people who will be using, wanting, consuming, or working with the Product/Results the Team is developing. Clients are interested in the capabilities (features, usability, speed, etc.) that are, or will be, delivered.

- **Customers**: The people who are, or will be, paying for the Product, or Results, the Team is producing. Customers are interested in schedules, budgets, costs, delivery dates, ROI, NPV, Investment and Sales Opportunities, and so on.

- **Subject Matter Experts (SMEs)**: People, external to the Team, who will act as 'honorary' Team Members when needed. These are people with competencies (knowledge and/or skills) that the Team needs, but do not exist on the Team itself. These people could be from any Stakeholder group, and their competencies could assist Production, Scrum Mastering, or Product Ownership.

Note: *These Stakeholder groups are neither independent nor mutually exclusive; the Stakeholder community is often a mess. We name these groups in order to help you make sense of this mess. For example:*

- *The Team must be able to clarify what needs to be done with many different Stakeholders, but especially with the Business, Regulators, and Clients – or their surrogates. These clarifications need to be done in near-real-time, so that Product Ownership does not have to be the go-between.*
- *One particular thing we like to do in order to get help when we need it is to co-opt Clients who want a particular feature to become SMEs, who will then work with the Team to develop that feature;*
- *Some People are both Customers and Clients, but they should play one role at a time – we don't want to see 'money people' in the Team room with the developers; and*

- *Many Organizations operate under complex Regulatory Regimens; Regulators produce standards, rules, and regulations... that can effect either what is built (e.g., it must be bi-lingual), how it is built (e.g., the Code must be completely protected by Tests), or both.*

We talk a lot about self-organization in Scrum, but that doesn't mean that Teams can ignore their Stakeholders... My 'off the record' definition of a Stakeholder is "somebody you ignore at your peril."

The (Scrum) Team

There is only one Team in Scrum, and that is the Scrum Team. A Scrum Team (commonly called the "Team") is a small, co-located, self-organized, self-contained, value-driven, group of full-time **Team Members** (including their SMEs on an as-needed basis) who are organized around a Mission. Let me define these terms:

- **Mission**: A short statement of why the Team exists – what it does, for whom, and why – the Mission is often obvious from looking at the Team's name – examples include *"Develop and Maintain the XYZ System"*, *"Project ABC"*, or *"Acme Construction Plumbing Team"*;

- **Small**: The Team must be small enough to remain nimble and large enough to complete significant work during a Sprint; typically this means that a Team has between three and nine Team Members – the 'sweet spot' for software development seems to be around five;

- **Co-Located**: Team Members must be co-located (at least virtually) so that they can talk to other Team Members within seconds/minutes, rather than hours/days.

- **Self-Organized**: A self-organized team is one that chooses how best to accomplish its work, rather than being directed (micro-managed) by others outside the team.

- **Self-Contained**: A self-contained (also called cross-functional) team is one that contains all the knowledge and skills necessary to accomplish its objectives and goals. In real life, this may require Subject Matter Experts

(SMEs) who are *not*, actually, full-time Team Members.

- **Full-Time**: Each Team Member belongs to a single Team. However, the Team, because it is self-organized, may 'loan out' one or more of its Team Members to work elsewhere as a Subject Matter Expert. In general, when there are multiple Teams involved, an individual Team Member may work on two Teams – a 'home' Team (the one he/she belongs to) and an 'away' Team (the one he/she visits)…

- **Value-Driven**: The Team Members value working together; they are constantly improving themselves, their Team, their environment, and their tools; and they strive to live up to **Values** that they – or their Organization – believe are important.

Notes:

1) There are many ways we can express values, and many different values we could have. The values the Team Members strive to meet could be things like:

- *Let's all be REAL (Responsible, Ethical, Accountable, Loyal) to each other;*

- *We believe in Honor, Courage, and Commitment (US Marines);*

- *Team Members should embody and live by the values of commitment, courage, focus, openness, and respect (Scrum Guide);*
- *Or any other set of values the Team is willing to believe in…*

2) *One collection of Values that we like is called the* **Team Values**, *which is an extension of the Scrum Values:*

Openness	*There should be no secrets between/amongst Team Members about things relevant to the work and their ability to do the work.*
Focus	*Everything the Team does must have a focus, and the Team Members must focus on what is important in everything they do.*
Commitment	*Team Members commit to each other, to the Team's goals, to be ethical, and to the Product itself.*
Respect	*Team Members believe that people are always doing the best they can do at any given moment.*
Courage	*Team Members must have the courage to make reality visible,*

Courage (cont.)	*do the right thing, and work on tough problems.*
Visibility	*Team Members make the current state of the Team's Product / Results visible to each other, Stakeholders and the Business.*
Humor	*Everyone needs a sense of humor; if we can't laugh at some of the things we do, we'd have to cry.*
Accountability	*Everyone is ultimately answerable for their work or decisions; anyone can be 'held to account' for what he or she does.*

The **Work Items** the Scrum Team works on are called **Stories**, and as the Team completes the Stories, they produce Results in an iterative and incremental manner, thus providing opportunities for meaningful feedback from Stakeholders. While they are doing their work – when they have **Work In Progress (WIP)** – they should *"do their due diligence and use an appropriate Standard of Care to do their work, without lollygagging or gold-plating."* which will (as Project Management training will teach you) maximize the Team's sustainable throughput.

There are no internal named 'technical' roles on a Team — they are all called, simply, Team Members, Developers, Plumbers,

Painters, or whatever is appropriate. Two of these Team Members have additional responsibilities/accountabilities – the Team Facilitator (TF) and the Team Captain (TC), which I define here (more detailed descriptions to follow):

- **Team Facilitator (TF)**: The Team Member who facilitates the Team's self-organization in order to help them do their work and remove their impediments; and
- **Team Captain (TC)**: The Team Member who is accountable to the Business for maximizing the value of the Team's Work.

Note: *Many people like to refer to the Team Facilitator and the Team Captain as the 'Scrum Master' and 'Product Owner', respectively. However, as we'll see in the next few sections, both Scrum Mastering and Product Ownership have multiple facets (different sub-roles) that belong to the Business Organization as a whole, and the TC and TF are the only two sub-roles that are* **required** *to actually be on the Scrum Team.*

Both the Team Facilitator and Team Captain are members of the self-organizing Scrum Team; they are Team Members with additional responsibilities, they should be thought of as Team Members 'wearing their TC and FC hats'. Because the Scrum Team is self-organized, they are available to help with Development Work, just as the other Team Members are available to help the TF and TC with Scrum Mastering and Product Ownership, respectively.

In fact, on some Scrum Teams, either the TC or SM (or both) may not be particular people; they are 'self-organized' on an as-needed basis. That is, when a Team Captain (or Scrum Master) is needed (outside the Team) for some reason, the Team selects a Representative to wear the 'TC (or SM) hat' for the required purpose.

It must be understood that putting these people on the Team is NOT a way to introduce management onto the Team. All Team Members need to work together constantly in order to do their work and produce the necessary Results – this is why they are together... I repeat... they are together because the work demands it, not as a way to introduce some sort of micro-management onto the Team.

Scrum Mastering

There are three roles involved in Scrum Mastering, including the Team Facilitator mentioned above. Each of these roles is a servant-leadership role, enabling and empowering people to do their jobs. Each of them is responsible for ensuring Scrum is understood and properly applied. Here are their definitions, their "One Big Thing". *(Note: some of the terms used here will be defined later in this handbook.)*

- **Team Facilitator (TF)**: The Team Member who facilitates the Team Members' self-organization (on a daily basis) to help them 1) do their work, 2) remove their **Impediments** to progress, and 3) achieve their Team's **Kaizen**, which is an improvement goal. Every Team must have a Team Facilitator, who is often a technical contributor, as well.

- **Agile Coach (AC)**: A person who works with the Scrum Team to help them improve their skills. The skills might be technical or non-technical, and improvements are typically achieved through training and/or mentoring. The Agile Coach often works with the Team Facilitator to: 1) help the Team Members understand, implement, and improve their use of Scrum and agility; and 2) help the Team identify its Kaizen every Sprint. Every Team must have access to an Agile Coach as needed; this usually requires one Agile Coach for every 2-10 Teams, with five being the 'sweet spot'.

- **Change Agent (CA)**: A person who helps the Organization adopt, implement, and sustain Scrum, and understand how best to support and work with Scrum Teams – this includes organizational design. There needs to be at least one Change Agent per Organization. The Change Agent is usually also an Agile Coach (with expertise in organizational behavior), and is considered the 'senior Scrum Master' in the Organization.

Scrum Mastering provides many other services to the Team and the Organization. Here is a list of additional responsibilities with indications of which Scrum Mastering roles would/could/should be involved *(Note: these responsibilities are 'lifted' directly from the Scrum Guide)*.

Scrum Mastering Responsibility	**TF**	**AC**	**CA**
Helping people understand which of their interactions with the Scrum Team are helpful and which aren't	X	X	X
Creating interactions that maximize the value created by the Scrum Team	X	X	X
Finding techniques for managing the Team's work effectively	X	X	
Helping the Organization understand the need for clear and concise statements of work		X	X
Helping the Scrum Team understand the need for clear and concise statements of work	X	X	
Helping the Organization understand planning in an agile environment			X

Scrum Mastering Responsibility	TF	AC	CA
Coaching the Team in self-organization and teamwork, including swarming	X	X	
Helping the Team to create high-quality Results	X		
Facilitating Scrum events as requested or needed	X	X	X
Coaching the Team in organizational environments in which Scrum is not yet fully adopted and understood	X	X	X
Leading and coaching the Organization in its Scrum adoption			X
Planning Scrum implementations within the Organization		X	X
Helping Stakeholders understand and enact Scrum and agility	X	X	X
Causing change that increases the productivity of the Scrum Team	X		
Working with other Scrum Masters to increase the effectiveness of the application of Scrum in the organization	X	X	X
Helping the Team acquire or deepen specific skills		X	
Ensuring the Organization is taking steps to develop and sustain necessary expert skills			X

This is a good list of responsibilities for the Scrum Mastering roles, but it incomplete. You will find other responsibilities for these roles as you continue reading this Handbook.

Note:

1) These three Scrum Mastering roles can be covered in different ways:

1) On mature Teams it is common for Team Facilitation to be done by 'everybody' on the Team as a self-organization issue. When the Team Facilitator is needed outside the Team, the Team selects and sends a representative.

2) It is common for some (or all) Team Facilitators to also be Agile Coaches. In this case, we refer to this combined role as a Facilitator/Coach (FC). These people are their own Team's Facilitator and Coach, and may also coach other Teams or their Facilitators. One or more of these FCs may also be Organizational Change Agents. Being one of these 'do everything' Scrum Masters could cause 'overloading' problems – their own Team's Facilitation could suffer – and they may need 'deputy' Team Facilitators (one of the Technical members of the Team) to pick up the load.

3) It is common for the Change Agent to also be the lone Agile Coach, if the Organization is relatively small (fewer than ten Teams). In this case, it is probable that each Team's Facilitator is also a technical contributor.

In any case, the people who play these roles must collaborate closely in order to be aligned on, and perform, their functions.

2) *The Change Agent helps identify needed changes in process, practices, and organizational design – which include changes in both Structure and Governance. The reason the Change Agent does this is to improve the Organization's Culture to be more accepting and supporting of Scrum and agility. The optimizing goals for the Organization should be: 1) to maximize its ability to change, and 2) to help it find high-value Items that need to be worked on. Often, the Change Agent will work with the Agile Actuary to evaluate proposed Organizational Design changes in an analytical way.*

Product Ownership

There are four Product Ownership roles, including the Team Captain mentioned above. Each of these roles is involved in producing Results that make Stakeholders 'happy' and, collectively, they span the range from creating visions and goals, to delivery management, to deciding what the Scrum Teams should do next. Here are their definitions, their "One Big Thing". *(Note: some of the terms used here will be defined later in this handbook.)*

- **Team Captain (TC)**: The Team Member who is accountable to the Business (often represented by a single Business Owner) for maximizing the value of the **Team's Work**. Each Team must have its own Team Captain to 'call the plays' about what work the Team should do next.

- **Business Owner (BO)**: A person who is accountable to Stakeholders for ordering a **Results Backlog** in order to maximize the value of delivered **Results**. We expect Business Owners to work with their Stakeholders (including **Product Champions**) to determine which Results should be delivered, and why.

- **Product Champion (PC)**: A type of Business Owner whose Results Backlog represents a *single* Product. The Product Champion owns the Product Vision, represents this Product's Clients and Customers to the Organization, and provides/identifies subject matter expertise to the Organization to aid in development and reviews.

- **Agile Actuary (AA)**: A professional who does qualitative and quantitative analysis to help Business Owners mitigate risk, support decision-making, evaluate options, and produce the **Delivery Forecast**. We would expect each Product to have its own Delivery Forecast (estimated Delivery Dates and Costs) along with an associated Agile Actuary.

The first three roles (Team Captain, Business Owner, and Product Champion) are 'ownership' roles (their job is to make prioritization decisions), while the Agile Actuary is a more technical role. Their responsibilities are tightly linked, and all impact the Scrum Teams. In particular, these roles interact to:

- Assure that the Work the Teams do is necessary to develop the Results that will be delivered to Stakeholders, and that the Teams understand both the Work and the Results to an appropriate level of detail;

- Assure that the expected scope of the Deliverable Results is consistent with the appropriate Delivery Forecast, that the Teams understand the expected scope of each Deliverable Result, and that the Teams are not overly influenced by the predictions of the Delivery Forecast;

- Assure that the predictions of the Delivery Forecast adapt to stay in alignment with the realities of the Work as they become visible, and that the Delivery Forecast is used to establish realistic delivery expectations with the Stakeholders; and

- Assure that Product Ownership uses *informed* decision-making; in particular, that the Agile Actuaries 1) identify indicators and metrics to aid decision-making, 2) work with Teams to collect observations and data, and 3) analyze the data and prepare advice for the Business Owners, Product Champions, Team Captains, and Change Agents.

Note: *The relationships between the people playing these roles are very important, as they, the Teams, and the Stakeholders, must be in alignment about what Results are to be delivered, and what work is needed to produce those Results.*

The best way to stay aligned is if all four Product Ownership roles are played by the same person – as is required by both Scrum$_P$ *and Scrum*$_G$*. This can, and has, happened. It's rare, though, and usually requires a one-team Organization with its Team Captain playing all the roles. Some Organizations have spread this single Team Captain across several Teams and made this work; I think this is because this common Team Captain is actually the Business Owner for each of the Teams, and the individual Teams are self-organizing their Team Captain as needed. And, of course, since this situation usually happens when there is only a single product, this Business Owner is actually the Product's Champion.*

More often than not, however, the roles are dispersed throughout the Organization in some way. In a large Organization there could be multiple development Scrum Teams doing the work, multiple Product Champions representing Products for different sets of Stakeholders, and Business Owners holding it all together, making sure value (to the Business) is being maximized. They must all be in alignment about 1) what is being built, and 2) the flow of work within the system. This alignment is achieved through collaboration and accountability, and puts a huge burden on the Organization's Scrum Masters, who must work with – and advise – the Product Ownership about how to do this.

So, here is some guidance about these issues…

1) *Each Team Captain is the* **only** *person in the Organization who decides what work his or her Team should do next (and this decision should be the result of conversations with appropriate Team Members, SMEs, Business Owners, Product Champions, and others). Many people may be involved in figuring out what* **should** *be worked on next, but the Team Captain is accountable for the actual decision of what* **will** *be worked on next. The Team Captain* **owns** *the* **Work Backlog**, *and the Team isn't allowed to act on what anyone else says.*

2) *Each Business Owner* **owns** *his or her* **Results Backlog** *and is the* **only** *person in the Organization who decides the prioritization of the Results in the Results Backlog. Many people, including Product Champions and Stakeholders,*

may have opinions about what the prioritization ***should*** *be, but the Business Owner is accountable for the actual decision. The Business Owner is accountable to prioritize the Results Backlog to maximize value to the Business.*

3) *Each Product should have a Product Champion (PC) who embraces multiple accountabilities:*

- *The PC is accountable to the Product's Clients for the capabilities and features that are (or will be) delivered;*
- *The PC is accountable to the Product's Customers for the Delivery Forecast (cost and schedule) for producing the Product (this usually involves the Agile Actuary);*
- *The PC (as a Business Owner) is accountable to the Business Organization to 'make money' on the project;*
- *The PC is accountable to the Regulators for 'following the rules', and*
- *The PC is accountable to the development Scrum Teams for providing (either personally or through SMEs) the business expertise that is needed.*

4) *A Scrum Team can be doing work for one or more Product Champions; having more than one Product for a single Team is the most common scaling problem we have. When there is more than one PC, there needs to be a Business Owner who 'sorts out' the conflicting prioritizations; this BO could be the Team Captain, or external to the Team. In any case, it makes no difference from the Team's perspective; they are completely focused on what their Team Captain wants them to do Now and Next. Here are a few different versions of this decision-making flow:*

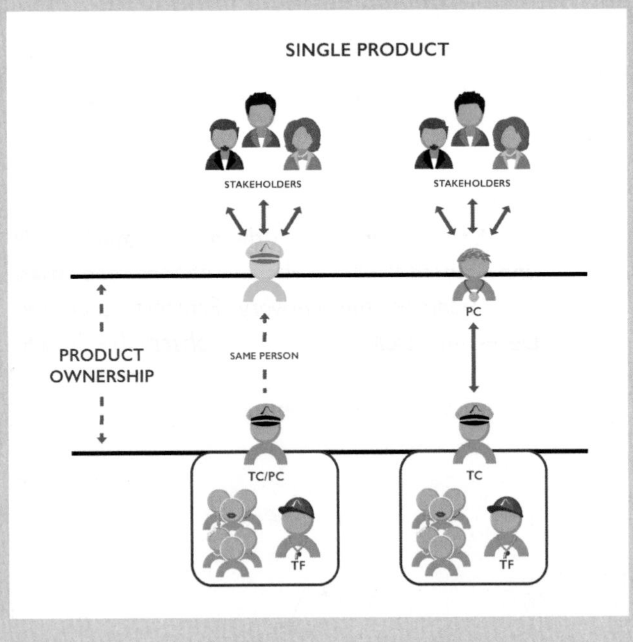

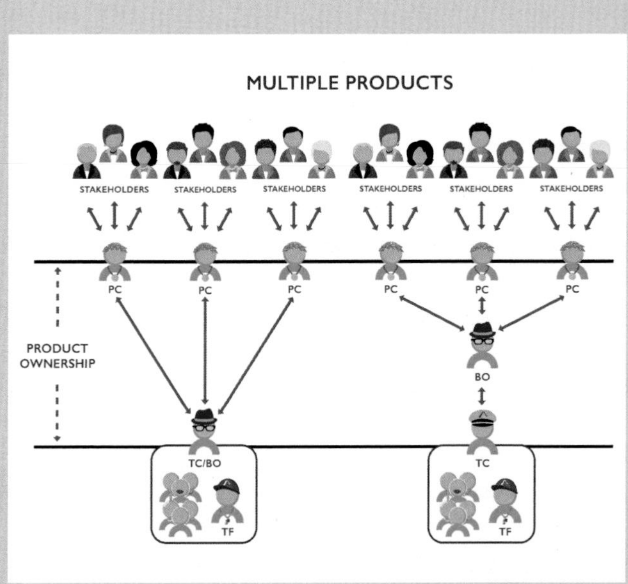

5) *The Agile Actuary is an advisor who qualitatively and quantitatively evaluates options and risks, and produces the Delivery Forecast (predicted Dates and Dollars) based on observable Reality. The Agile Actuary knows what data to collect and understands, trusts, and believes the data. The AA's mantra is "don't tell me a story, show me some data!" We have found that many Organizations (and Business Owners) like to tell stories rather than use data, and that's why they need an Agile Actuary along for the ride.*

6) *The Agile Actuary helps Business Owners and Product Champions use data to make 'tough decisions' about options and risks, and works with them to produce Delivery Forecasts and establish realistic delivery expectations with the Stakeholders. The Agile Actuary may advise Business Owners and Product Champions about 'what the numbers mean', but they (the 'Owners') make any decisions that need to be made.*

7) *The Agile Actuary usually acts as an appendage of a Business Owner; by combining a Product Champion with an Agile Actuary we get a Delivery Owner (DO) – who 'owns' a delivery of a particular Product to its Stakeholders. Sometimes, when a Business Owner works with an Agile Actuary, we call the combination a Business Manager (BM), who is driving prioritizations with data.*

8) *When multiple Scrum teams are collectively driven by a single Business Owner (acting as the Team Captain of a Leadership Team, for example), the Agile Actuary is usually a member of that Leadership Team who can be used as a Subject Matter Expert to help evaluate risks within the organization.*

9) *The Agile Actuary is an expert in qualitative and quantitative analysis to support decision-making.The Change Agent suggests options for improvement of*

processes, practices, and organizational design. We expect the two of them to work together to analyze these options in order to provide good advice for the people playing Product Ownership roles.

10) Since the Scrum Team's basic job is to "do its due diligence and use an appropriate Standard of Care to do its work, without lollygagging or gold-plating," it is inappropriate (in fact, it is probably harmful) for the expectations created by the Delivery Forecast to be available to Team Members (with the possible exception of the Team Captain, but even that could be risky). Measuring the Team to help it learn more about how it could improve its work could be a good thing; however, if the Team knows that it is considered slow, expensive, late, or otherwise feels pressure to 'improve', this will ***always*** *create a tension to compromise the appropriate Standard of Care. This* ***cannot*** *be allowed…*

Ok, this is enough about Product Ownership for now. You will continue to find other responsibilities for these Product Ownership roles as you continue reading this Handbook.

Artifacts

Backlog

The work of a Team is driven by a Backlog, which is *"a list of Work Items that represents everything that anyone interested in the Team's Results or Process has thought is needed or would be a good idea."* The Backlog is always a living document, and contains Work Items the Team might do, or Results (Deliverables) Stakeholders might want. There are several different parts of the Backlog, and I will discuss them below the picture.

Here are the parts of the Backlog.

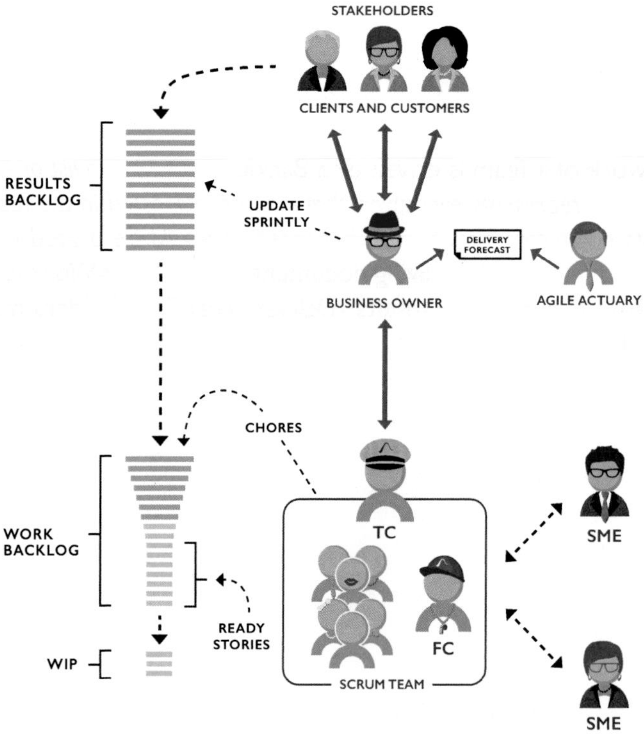

Figure 6: Parts of the Backlog

Results Backlog

The Results Backlog belongs to the Business Owner *(or a Product Champion, in the case that the Results Backlog represents a single Product, when it could be called a Product Backlog)*, and is a prioritized list of Results (Deliverables) that the Business Owner hopes to deliver to Clients. The Results Backlog is often accompanied by a Delivery Forecast that predicts when the Results will be delivered, and how much they will cost.

- The Business Owner works with the Clients to assure that the Results are what the Clients need. The Results (Deliverables) are often **Epics** — big, chunky, Work Items with ill-defined Acceptance Criteria.

- The Business Owner and Team Captain collaborate to determine which **Stories** (small, well-defined, Work Items) should be extracted from these Epics and 'passed down' to the Team's Work Backlog so that the Team can work on them.

- (if necessary) the Agile Actuary helps the Business Owner produce the Delivery Forecast for the Customers. The Delivery Forecast will normally be updated every Sprint based on data from the **Progress Review** to assure that the Results Backlog and the Delivery Forecast are 'in sync' and represent the realities of development.

Work Backlog

The Work Backlog belongs to the Team Captain, and consists of the Stories that the Team expects to be asked to work on 'soon'. These Stories are of two types:

- **Capabilities** that the Business Owner wants the Team to produce in order to deliver Results (Deliverables) to external Stakeholders; these are the stories that were 'passed down' from the Results Backlog.

- **Chores** added by the Team; work the Team must do that does not directly provide deliverable Results (e.g., 'do the dishes', 'clean up the code', or 'train the team'); the Chores typically include the Team's Kaizen.

The Team Backlog is constantly being Refined by the Team *(Backlog Refinement is described later in this Handbook)* so that there is always a subset of the Team Backlog that is immediately actionable, or **Ready** to be worked on. Typically, a Story is Ready when the Team knows the Story's Acceptance Criteria, what Standard Of Care to use for the Story, and which Subject Matter Experts they will be working with.

The Work In Progress (WIP)

The Work In Progress belongs to the Team and consists of the Stories the Team is actively working on, along with their associated **Tasks**. The Team often uses a **WIP Limit** to help manage bottlenecks in development as the Team does its work.

Note:

1) You may be asking: "Where are the Product Backlog and Sprint Backlog? That's what I'm used to seeing!" Well, they are there too. In Scrum$_H$ we emphasize the Continuous Flow of work involved in Development, and think of the Sprint as being an interrupt of that Continuous Flow. In particular, we don't think of the Sprint as a Container of Stories. Unfortunately, our tools often treat the Sprint as if it were a Container of Stories… If you have to deal with such a tool, you can do that, with the following definitions:

- ***Sprint Backlog**: The Sprint Backlog consists of the Work In Progress along with the Ready Stories that have been brought into the Sprint, whether they are committed to, forecasted to be worked on, or whatever.*

- ***Product Backlog**: The Product Backlog consists of the Results Backlog along with the portion of the Work Backlog that has not been moved to the Sprint Backlog.*

2) Also, you may have noticed that there are three types of Work Items that are mentioned: Epics, Stories, and Tasks, with the following basic descriptions:

- *Epics are big things that the Business Owner*

talks to Stakeholders about. Basically, an Epic is 1) something that the Stakeholders think of as a single unit of work, or deliverable, and 2) is too big for the Team to get to "Done" all at once;

- *Stories are small things that are either 1) passed down to Teams (Capabilities) or 2) created by the Teams themselves (Chores). Basically, Stories are things that the Team thinks of as a single unit of work that can be "Done" by working with SMEs; and*

- *Tasks are things that the Team creates in order to organize and do the work.*

We have found that people like to argue about what these words mean and, in general, worry about them way too much. The main importance of these words is that they give the Team a vocabulary to use when discussing the size of the work – these sizes become the focus of conversations.

For example, there may be a big mismatch between the 'size' of the Results the Stakeholders want, and the 'size' of the Capabilities the Team can consume. For example, a Result the Stakeholders want may be like "I want a new House", and the Capabilities the Team is capable of dealing with may be like "Paint this wall"; it may require thousands of Stories to implement a single Deliverable Result. The Business Owner and

Team Captain are required to collaborate in order to extract and 'pass down' Stories to the Team, and they may not be capable of this without additional analytic help – which must come from somewhere. This is actually a scaling problem because the system, as it stands, does not have the capacity to consume the work they are being asked to consume. Anyway, you gotta talk about it…

3) *The Backlogs define a flow of work from the Stakeholders to the Team; this flow should be viewed from a lean perspective. From that Point of View, the Work Backlog is the Inventory that is feeding the WIP. Since Inventory should be minimized, the Work Backlog should be replenished slowly, and only because there is a 'pull' caused by work in the WIP getting "Done". In other words, Work flows because getting work "Done" 'pulls' work down to the Team; this should be the driver, not the need for Stakeholders to 'push' the work down to the Team. Pull not Push…*

Increment

As the Team completes each Capability Story it produces Results (proposed and partial Deliverables) that require meaningful feedback from appropriate Stakeholders. The collection of accumulated Results is called the **Increment**; the increment should always be "Done" and in reviewable condition.

***Note**: The fact that the Increment is composed of "proposed and partial Deliverables" does not necessarily mean that we are building our Deliverable a piece at a time – that would be incremental, not agile, development. It does mean that the Increment is capable of eliciting meaningful feedback from Stakeholders that helps the Team and Business Owner determine what to do next.*

- *One of the things the Business Owner could do next is decide to deliver the Increment. Another could be to add something to the Increment. Another could be to modify the Increment. Another could be to completely change directions and build something else. You never know...*

- *There is an excellent video on this topic from Henrik Kniberg, "Making sense of MVP (Minimum Viable Product)", which can be found on YouTube. I recommend that every Business Owner watch it.*

Description of "Done"

For the Increment to be "Done", each Story that was involved in producing the Results included in the Increment needs to be "Done". For any particular Story, its definition of "Done" is the *"shared understanding, between the Team and the Story's Stakeholders, of what it means for the Story to be complete."* This is not as simple as it seems, as there are many potential Stakeholders for a Story: there are Clients who are interested in Capabilities, Team Members who are interested in Chores, Customers who are interested in Costs, and you can't forget the Regulators, whose needs must be satisfied, as well.

Typically, this understanding has two parts:

1. **Acceptance Criteria (AC)**: the *objective* criteria the Team will use to determine whether or not the Story achieves the Value the Stakeholders expect or need – this is what will be reviewed by the Stakeholders. In software development, for functional Stories, this is often a description of an **Acceptance Test**. If there is no objective test to use; the Story is usually time-boxed – the Acceptance Criteria is met when the time-box expires.

2. **Standard of Care (SoC)**: the description of the *objective* criteria the Team will use to determine whether or not work on the Story meets quality, process, or regulatory standards and constraints – as opposed to providing Value to Clients. The Standard of Care is used to 'guarantee' that the Results meet Regulatory Constraints and have sufficient technical quality to be releasable.

A Story's Acceptance Criteria are usually negotiated and discussed with its Clients or surrogates, while the Standard of Care is a bit more complicated. Some parts of the SoC could come from outside the Organization, through contractual obligations, a Regulatory body, or some such. Other parts of the SoC could be part of the conventions, standards, or guidelines of the Organization, and some could be developed by the Scrum Team itself. In any case, each Story the Team works on must have a Standard of Care and, when working with software, all Scrum Teams working in the same codebase, doing the same or similar Stories, must use the same Standard of Care for them.

Note: *Many Stories can have the same Standard of Care; these Stories are said to be of the same* **Storyotype**. *Storyotypes can be very useful because they capture common Standards of Care that can be reused as necessary. Some Organizations or Scrum Teams use the same Storyotype for all stories; for example, when all Stories produce Code for the same Product. In general, though, there need to be many Storyotypes to cover all the different types of work (Stories) the Team does. When using Storyotypes, we expect that they will be improved over time in order to provide higher quality Results more efficiently and effectively.*

In any case, no matter what the Story, the Team makes the determination whether or not a Story is "Done"; this is not something that occurs outside the Team. In fact, the determination that the story is "Done" is part of the Story itself. This is important, and an extension of the requirement that the Team is self-contained – that the Team has all the skills and knowledge to get its work completed.

In a Regulated environment that requires formal Inspections, there could be a 'final Inspection' that happens outside the Team (and is thus not part of the Story's "Done"), but this final Inspection does not relieve the Team from doing an internal inspection to verify that it is "Done" with the Story.

> **Note**: *Since the Team Captain is accountable for the Team's Results, it is quite common for the Team to have a 'ceremony' that indicates that the Team Captain is taking ownership of a Story's "Doneness". For example, when using a Storyboard, the Team Captain may be the Team Member who physically moves the Story to the "Done" column…*

Delivery Forecast

The Agile Actuary helps the Business Owner develop the Delivery Forecast, which is an artifact that predicts Delivery Dates and Costs for the Results being produced. This is an optional artifact, and proves to be necessary in many contexts. There is no established content or form for the Delivery Forecast; each Organization must determine its own needs and development practices.

Note: *The Delivery Forecast can be something as simple as a predicted Delivery Date based on Velocity, to something as complex as a Project Plan comparing Baselines and Actuals to calculate Earned Value Metrics that support predictions of Cost, Scope, and Schedule. In any case, there are two things to keep in mind:*

1) *The Delivery Forecast should be based on Data, not hope. The Scrum Team telling you they will deliver on time is not Data. Telling the Team what it will deliver, and when, is not Data.*

2) *You should be very wary of making the Delivery Forecast visible to the Scrum Team (except, perhaps, the Team Captain), as it can be harmful. If the Team knows what the delivery expectations are, there are two 'bad' things that could happen:*

- *If Team Members feel that they are 'beating expectations', they may slow down (as a consequence of Parkinson's Law), causing problems later on, or*
- *If Team Members feel that they are 'too slow', they will often try to speed up – and they will likely compromise the Standard of Care to do so.*

Process

The Scrum Process has a fairly small collection of ceremonies, discussions, activities, or meetings. The purpose of these ceremonies is to have collaborative conversations, do work, sync-up, and make decisions. The overarching purpose of the Scrum Process is to help the Team surface useful information so that they can be agile by adapting to, and exploiting, opportunities to achieve Results. See the following diagram:

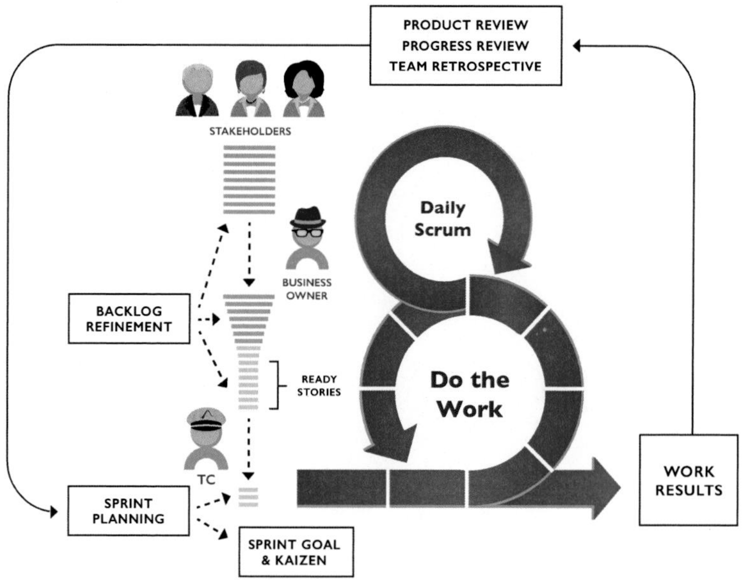

Figure 7: The Scrum Process

At its most basic, the Scrum Process can be thought of as a **Continuous Flow** of production work, with an interrupt every Sprint to allow for Feedback, Improvement, and Re-Planning.

Continuous Flow

Let me first describe the Continuous Flow, which is actually done day-by-day. Every day, the Scrum Team does the following things.

Daily Scrum

The Team has a Daily Scrum, when it self-organizes and plans its day. This discussion should take no more than 15 minutes. Typically, the Team discusses 1) its current state; 2) its progress towards its Sprint Goal, its Increment, and its Kaizen; and 3) the Impediments it's running into. This allows the Team to figure out what it hopes to do today. The result of the Daily Scrum is that the Team Members leave the Daily Scrum 'walking with a purpose' — they know what they're doing next — even though it could change in just a few minutes.

> ***Note**: Many people think that the Daily Scrum is all about the three questions: 1) What did you do? 2) What are you planning to do? and 3) What's standing in your way? Actually, these questions are only one of many ways to help determine the Team's current state, and many Teams do it in different ways. For example, some Teams talk about the state of the Stories in the WIP, rather than what people are working on…*
>
> *What is important is that the Team Members use the*

Daily Scrum to understand 1) where they are, 2) where they want to be, and 3) what they are going to do today to help them get there…

Do Work

The Team Does Work, which means:

- The Team swarms with its Subject Matter Experts in order to get Stories that are in the WIP to "Done".
- As Stories get to "Done", the Team Captain determines which Ready Stories should be moved from the Work Backlog to the WIP,
- The Team makes advances on its Kaizen, and
- The Team discusses and removes Impediments.

Maintain the Results Backlog

The Stakeholders, Business Owner, and appropriate Product Champions (if necessary) maintain the Results Backlog, by

- Adding/Removing/Changing the Deliverables in the Results Backlog, and
- Ordering/Re-Ordering the Results Backlog.

Backlog Refinement

The Team does Backlog Refinement (as necessary) with its Subject Matter Experts and its Business Owner, to assure that there are Ready Stories in the Work Backlog. These discussions are more-or-less continuous, with the total amount of Refinement taking no more that 10% of the Sprint. Refinement includes:

- Extracting Capabilities from the Results Backlog to the Work Backlog, usually when the Work Backlog gets a 'little low';
- Adding necessary Chores to support those Capabilities;
- Ordering/Re-Ordering the Stories (both Capabilities and Chores) in the Work Backlog; and
- Refining the Stories near the *top/front* of the Work Backlog to make them Ready to be worked on. A Ready Story is one that is immediately actionable by the Team, and making a Story Ready typically includes:
    - Determining what "Done" means for the Story; defining and finalizing its
        - Acceptance Criteria, such as a functional test or time-box, and
        - Standard of Care, defining Quality (and other) Constraints,
    - Splitting 'large' Stories into 'small' Stories as necessary,

- Sizing the Stories, if necessary, to support gathering data to update the Delivery Forecast, and
- Determining which Subject Matter Experts need to be available to work on the Story.

Note:

1) *Since we are thinking of a Scrum Team's work as a continuous flow with a Sprintly interrupt, we are not overly upset if a Story's work overflows to the next Sprint. We just need to leave the Story in a 'good state' so that we can restart work on it when the next Sprint Starts, should we decide to do so.*

   The Team is also not worried about how much will get done in the Sprint. The Team is focused on getting work to "Done" without lollygagging or gold-plating; it is not focused on the end of the Sprint. When the Sprint ends, the current Increment (collection of "Done" work) gets reviewed. The Team is always looking for both useful feedback and ways to improve.

   If something really, truly, has to get done by a given date, the Business Owner and Team Captain must make sure they have plenty of buffer built in so that the Story's Standard of Care does not need to be compromised to meet the date. The basic guidance is: "if you want it soon, you better start it early…"

2) The Sprint is often used as a common cadence within Organizations to:

- *Coordinate the integration of the Results of many Teams, and*
- *Instill good habits and behaviors. Once a Team has matured and developed such behaviors, it should continue to use the Sprint Interrupt as a cadence for continuous, ongoing, improvement.*

3) In order to minimize inventory for the Scrum Team, which would be recommended when using lean thinking, you could use a limit on the number of Capabilities that are represented in the Work Backlog. That is, you may make a practice of moving a Capability from the Results Backlog to the Work Backlog only when a (refined) Capability has been completed, and all its extracted Stories have been "Done". In other words, move work to the Team when the Team getting work "Done" 'pulls' it down; don't try to 'push' work down to the Team.

Interrupt Each Sprint

At the end of the Sprint the Team has four Ceremonies/Events/Discussions/Meetings in order to allow for Feedback, Improvement, and Re-Planning.

Product Review

At the end of a Sprint, the Team, the Business Owner, and appropriate Product Champions (if necessary) have a Product Review with Clients in order to obtain Meaningful Feedback for the Team about the Team's Results (proposed and partial Deliverables). This is at most a three-hour discussion for a four-week Sprint, and proportionally shorter for shorter Sprints. This discussion is 'owned' by the Business Owner, and consists of discussions driven by questions like: *"What do you like about what we did?"*, *"What don't you like?"*, *"What would you like to change?"*, and *"What would you like to see next?"* The whole Scrum Team, the Business Owner, the Product Champions, and the Clients should be involved in these discussions.

Note:

1) This discussion is about getting feedback on the Team's Results; the idea is for the Business Owner to gain the feedback he/she needs in order to prioritize the Capabilities that the Team will work on in the next Sprint. Sometimes, there are discussions about the work itself, or the Standard of Care, and those discussion are owned by the Team Captain.

The Product Review is not the only feedback the Team should be getting from your Clients. In fact, we often use the Review as a 'recruitment exercise' to get people to come work with the Team as Subject Matter Experts. I've often used a sentence like the following: "I can see that you'd like this changed; could you please help us get it right in the next Sprint? Could you send somebody?"

2) *Since a Team can be working on multiple Products, each with its own set of Stakeholders, there may be a need to have multiple Product Reviews – to review multiple products. The main point is that the Team must receive meaningful feedback about its Results every Sprint; it is not about the meeting, it is about the feedback...*

   For example, I once had two major Clients (call them WalWay and SafeMart) who received their own tailored versions of our Product. It would be ludicrous to think we could get them in the same room at the same time, and we tried two different strategies at different times:

   - *We held two different reviews, one for each Client, and*
   - *We did a single review, and included our Salespersons who were their Product Champions.*

In the second case, the salespersons had to work as go-betweens, and this often led to additional Reviews (as Stories) within the next Sprint. Frankly, we never could decide which method produced better results…

Bottom Line: You've got to think about your Product Reviews; you've got to figure out how best to do them. They are not simply about 'following the process', they are about 'getting meaningful feedback'. You may need to have multiple meetings, do some of them as Stories within the Sprint, or whatever, in order to get this feedback.

In any case, you should keep them short; the total of ALL your Product Reviews should add up to no more than the appropriate amount of time (45 minutes per week of Sprint), and keeping them short will likely help turn them into the recruitment exercises I mentioned above.

Progress Review

The Team Captain, Business Owner, and Product Champions (augmented by the Agile Actuary) have a Progress Review with Customers about 'how the work is going' — information to help update the Delivery Forecast(s), evaluate risks, and set expectations with the Customers. This discussion should take no more than one-hour for a four-week Sprint, and proportionally shorter for shorter Sprints. This discussion is 'owned' by the Business Owner, and leverages the expertise of the Agile Actuary. The discussion is largely about risks, Dates, and Dollars. Discussions involve questions like: *"How fast are we going?"*, *"When will we be done?"*, *"What's going to jump up and bite us?"*, and *"How do we adapt Cost, Scope, and Schedule to match the realities we see?"*

Note: *Even though the Agile Actuary is heavily involved in this discussion, any changes in plans are owned by the Business Owner (or Product Champion). The Agile Actuary understands the relationship between Cost, Scope, and Schedule – and may offer options about how to keep them balanced and in sync – but any decisions about what to do (change Scope, get additional Funding, and so on) belong to Business Ownership.*

Since the Team could be working on multiple deliveries with multiple Delivery Forecasts and different Customers, there may need to be multiple Progress Reviews. As with the Product Reviews, you've got to figure out how best to do them. Because this is a Product Ownership thing, and need not involve the rest of the Team, is can easily be done during the Sprint. In any case, keep the total time of the Progress Reviews short, with a total amount of time maxed out at 15 minutes per week of Sprint. Basically, this is just an informational meeting, with the Agile Actuary supplying 'expert' advice about Dates and Dollars that will lead to further discussions about what to do…

Team Retrospective

The Scrum Team has a Retrospective at the end of a Sprint (facilitated by the Team Facilitator with possible support from a Agile Coach) in order to discuss and agree upon ways they could improve their Practices, teamwork, environment, or Organization for the next Sprint. This Discussion should take three-hours for a four-week Sprint, and proportionally shorter for shorter Sprints. This discussion is 'owned' by the Team Facilitator, and is driven by the questions: *"What did we do well"* and *"What could we improve?"* One result of the Retrospective should be to propose a Kaizen (or two) that could be worked on in the next Sprint.

Note: *The Retrospective is about Team improvement. Scrum expects a Team to do Kaizen, which is the process of continuous improvement, and to do this the team selects a Kaizen (one single improvement to work on) every Sprint. Technically, the choice of the Sprint's Kaizen is done during Sprint Planning, but finding potential Kaizens is part of the Retrospective.*

The last of these discussions 'between the Sprints' is actually the beginning of the next Sprint...

Sprint Planning

Sprint Planning is a discussion the Team has at the beginning of the Sprint in order to:

- Establish **Sprint End** (when the interrupt for the four Ceremonies will take place),
- Select a Kaizen to accomplish,
- Make sure there are enough Stories Ready or 'In Progress' so the Team can get back to work, and
- Determine a Sprint Goal.

Note:

1) Sprint End usually consists of dates and times for the Product and Progress Reviews. However, the Sprint End could also be state (or milestone) based. For example, the Sprint End could be defined by the following statements:

- *We'll have a review as soon as Randy can get a meeting with the Clients; or*
- *Let's review this thing after we finish these first four Stories.*

2) *There is no reason that all four Ceremonies need to be held at the same time; they just need to be held at least once a Sprint.*

   - *I have had teams that Retrospected every week, but had their Reviews every two weeks. It's about getting frequent meaningful feedback, not following a process.*

   - *When there are multiple Products involved, the Team will probably need multiple Reviews (both Product and Progress). Often, these Reviews will have to be held as Stories in the next Sprint.*

3) *Sprint Planning can be done in many ways: some like to get 'just enough' Stories as defined above; some like to fill the Sprint, some like to do two-pass planning; some do one-pass planning; and so on. Sprint Planning is certainly a 'self-organization thing'… Consequently, the length of Sprint Planning is highly variable. For two-week Sprints I have seen it as short as 15 minutes, and as long as four hours.*

   In Scrum 1.0, the Team's Sprint Commitment was usually to complete the Sprint Backlog. In Scrum 2.0 and Scrum 3.0, the Sprint Commitment is to a single Sprint Goal. This change in Sprint Commitment was made so that there will be 'wiggle room' for the Team to meet their commitment without being rushed and (possibly) compromise the Standard of Care.

4) *Even though the BO (or TC) may present the Team with an objective the BO (or TC) hopes the Team will meet, the Sprint Goal is what they are committed to – and it is determined by the Team. The Team can choose just about anything to be its Sprint Goal. Here are a few examples of appropriate Sprint Goals:*

   - *No head works alone this Sprint (a Goal about Process),*
   - *Bring the new people, Joe and Gina, up to speed (a Goal about the People),*
   - *Clean up Module ABC (a Goal about a Chore),*
   - *No 'cheating' on the Code Reviews (A goal about their Kaizen), or*
   - *Have a releasable version of <Buy an e-Ticket> (a Goal about the Product).*

Whatever the Sprint Goal is, the Team is actually committed to it; they will do 'anything they have to do' in order to meet it. The Sprint Goal is not aspirational – it's not a hope or dream – it is an actual commitment; it's something "that will be met within the Sprint" (Scrum Guide).

These are the ceremonies that happen every Sprint. Once a Sprint starts, we expect the Team to do work until the end of the Sprint, but they sometimes need to stop early.

Stopping a Sprint

There are two ways the Sprint can be stopped before its planned end.

Sprint Cancellation

The Team Captain may cancel a Sprint at any time, usually because the Business Owner requests it, often because the BO's objective for the Sprint isn't going to be met, or the objective is no longer what is needed. In any case, the Sprint's work is evaluated to see what can be kept, and whether or not a re-planning is called for. This is not considered abnormal, but is simply an agile reaction to something that has happened. It should not be considered a 'bad thing' – it is merely a 'thing.'

Abnormal Termination

Not only can the Team Captain cancel a Sprint at any time, but the Team Facilitator can stop the Sprint at any time at the behest of the Team – this is called an Abnormal Termination. The Abnormal Termination has been a part of Scrum from the very beginning, and it has always been a very important part of a Team's self-organization – the Team needs to have the power to cancel its own Sprint. If an Abnormal Termination is invoked, the Sprint is re-planned and all work in the Sprint is discarded, making it a 'very big deal'.

__Note__: The Abnormal Termination is rarely invoked; it is usually used as a threat. The threat of an Abnormal Termination alerts management (in a very noticeable way) that something is going wrong and needs to be addressed. The most common use of the threat of the Abnormal Termination is when Product Ownership is doing something the Team considers 'out of line'. In essence, the threat is saying 'if you don't play nice, we'll go on strike.'

In any case, Teams should not threaten to use the Abnormal Termination unless they are willing to actually use it. The Abnormal Termination is quite disruptive, but does give the Team the ability to re-start a Sprint with a clean slate.

SECTION 3

Glossary of Scrum Terms

Scrum uses many terms that are confusing to people, and many of these terms are used throughout this Handbook. This glossary presents many terms and phrases that have become 'standard' in the Scrum community, as well as a few that are introduced here. This is not a complete list!

Abnormal Termination - A cancellation of the Sprint by the Scrum Master at the behest of the Team. This is a self-organization 'thing' and is often threatened but seldom invoked – it is usually used by the Team as a way of saying *'you didn't play nice, so we are forcing a do-over.'*

Acceptance-Based Story - A Story whose 'doneness' is determined by Acceptance Criteria; the Effort an Acceptance-Based Story takes is a byproduct of getting to Done. *(see Time-Boxed Story)*

Acceptance Criteria - A description of the objective criteria the Team will use to determine whether or not a Story achieves the Value it represents. For functional Stories, this is usually a description of an Acceptance Test. *(see Story Agreement)*

Accountability - Everyone is ultimately answerable for their work or decisions; anyone can be 'held to account' for what he or she does. *(see Values)*

Accountable - The accountable person is the individual who is ultimately answerable for the activity or decision; the accountable person can be *held to account* for the results of the activity or the making of the decision. There can only be one person accountable for any particular activity or decision. Often confused with Responsible. *(see Responsible)*

Actionable Story - *(see Ready Story)*

Agile - 1) having a decision-making cycle tight enough to deal with complexity; 2) An umbrella term that encompasses a family of processes known for being 'agile' (Scrum, eXtreme Programming (XP),

DSDM, Crystal, Feature Driven Development, Agile2, Kanban, and others). *(see Agility)*

Agile Actuary - A professional who does qualitative and quantitative analysis to help Business Owners mitigate risk, support decision-making, evaluate options, and produce the Delivery Forecast. *(see Product Ownership)*

Agile Analysis - Any iterative and incremental method or practice that produces Epics and/or Stories for the Backlog.

Agile Coach - The person who works with the Team Facilitator to 1) help the Team Members understand, implement, and improve their use of Scrum and agility; and 2) help the Team identify its Kaizen every Sprint.

agility - The act of adapting to, and exploiting, the realities we see, as opposed to being predictive or plan-driven. Agility has two primary facets: Physical Agility and Mental Agility. *(see Physical Agility, Mental Agility)*

Agreement - *(see Story Agreement)*

Agreement-Based Planning - An alternative to capacity-driven methods for sprint planning. With Agreement-Based Planning Product Ownership and the Team work together to add stories to the Sprint, one at a time, until the Team agrees that the Sprint is 'full'. Things like who is available, technical debt, and the story's Doneness Agreement, are all taken into account, as they impact what the team can and cannot do.

Alignment - People are in alignment about something when their understandings of the essence of that something are consistent; we often say they "are on the same page". The primary goal of Product Ownership is to have Goals, Strategies, Plans, and Action in alignment from top to bottom – from Stakeholders to Production Team Members. (note: this concept was originally described by General Helmuth von Moltke (the elder) (1800-1891), and the German term for this concept is "Auftragsklärung")

Analysis Story - A Story that finds Items or Stories; a Story that conducts Agile Analysis. The most common Analysis Stories find functional Stories by one of various methods (working with SMEs, studying Change Requests, conducting Usability Analysis, etc.); however, there can also be risk analysis Stories (finding risks and fears that need be dealt with), process analysis Stories (finding process improvements), and so on. *(see Agile Analysis, Backlog Refinement)*

Architecturally Significant Story - A Functional Story that causes the Team to make an architectural decision, which is then validated by the fact that there is existing, working functionality using the decision. *(see Functional Story)*

Architecture - The collection of decisions about how a system will be built –from Grady Booch in the early 80's. *(see Architecturally Significant Story)*

Back Burner - Stories in the Backlog that are being refined to become Ready for Planning. Usually thought of as being Stories that are 'near the top (or front)' of the Backlog and *becoming* Ready. *(see Ready Story)*

Backlog - A list of Items that represents everything that anyone interested in the Team's Results or process has thought is needed or would be a good idea. It drives development and discussions with Stakeholders. *(see Results Backlog, Work Backlog)*

Backlog Item - *(see Item)*

Backlog Maintenance - *(see Backlog Refinement)*

Backlog Refinement - The process of extracting Stories from Epics and/or refining Stories to make them Ready. There could be Refinement Stories, Sessions, or both. (a*lso called Grooming, Backlog Maintenance or Story Time*)

Bug - 1) A simple change that does not require an acceptance test; examples include correcting a misspelling in a dialog box or moving an interface element on the screen; 2) Often used (incorrectly, in my view) as a synonym for Defect. *(see Defect)*

BuildUp - A BuildUp graph is any graph that shows the completion of Backlog as a function of Time. Many people call these BurnUp graphs. *(see BurnUp)*

BurnDown - A BurnDown graph is any graph that shows the amount of remaining Backlog (Items or Tasks) as a function of Time. Many people and tools use BurnDowns, but they have been largely deprecated from Scrum as they are inherently predictive, and not agile.

BurnUp - *(see BuildUp)*

Business Organization - The organization the Team belongs to, or works for. The Business Organization provides services the Team needs in order to exist, such as Human Resources, Logistics, Facilities, Contracting, Training, and so on.

Business Owner - A Product Ownership role that represents the person who is accountable to the Clients and the Business for maximizing the value of the Deliverable Results (the Product). *(see Product Ownership)*

Business Value (BV) - A property of an Item that simply indicates that some external Stakeholder wants it done; it is very hard to quantify, even though we continue to try to do so.

Cadence - *(see Rhythm)*

Cancelling a Sprint - The Product Owner may cancel a Sprint at any time, usually because the Sprint Goal isn't going to be met or because the Sprint Goal is no longer what is needed.

Capability - An Item that provides value to an external Stakeholder; an Item that has Business Value. *(compare to Chore)*

Capacity - An estimate or prediction of the rate that a Team or Organization *will be able* to develop Product; it is often used in Release Planning. Often confused with Velocity and WorkRate.

'Catch' Feedback - Feedback obtained by actively listening to responses from a stakeholder during review of an artifact (such as a completed story or product increment). *(see 'Pull' Feedback)*

Change Agent - The person who helps the Organization adopt Scrum and understand how best to support Scrum Teams - this includes good Organizational Design.

Chore - An Item that is done to provide value to the Team or Product, as opposed to an external Stakeholder; an Item whose value is other than Business Value. *(compare to Capability)*

Clean Code - 1) Code that is easy to change: that is extensible, modifiable, and maintainable. 2) Code that has little or no Technical Debt. *(see Technical Debt)*

CleanUp Story - A Story that *apologizes* to the Code Base about something bad that happened, and *promises* to fix it. It usually documents what is wrong and indicates what needs to be done to fix it. A Cleanup Story is a story that tells us where the mess is and what we have to do to clean it up.

Clients - The people who will be using, consuming, or working with the Product/Results the Team is developing.

Co-Located - A Team 'being co-located' means that its Team Members must be close enough together (either physically or virtually) that they can talk to each other within seconds/ minutes, rather than hours/days.

Code Complete - A Product Increment is code complete when the development team agrees that no entirely new source code (including automated tests) needs to be added.

Coding Story - A Story that has Code as its primary result.

Commitment - One of the least understood of the Team Values; the Team commits to living the Scrum Values and doing its due diligence to get Stories Done. It is often used as a synonym for Sprint Commitment. *(see Values)*

Complex Problem - Any problem that is too complicated for any one person to fully grok (understand deeply).

Continuous Flow - 1) Moving products through a production system without separating them into lots; 2) In Scrum, doing all work on an as-needed, just-in-time, basis, with each chunk of work being completed without interruptions. The work the Scrum Team does every day includes the Daily Scrum, Production, Maintaining the Results Backlog, and Backlog Refinement.

Coordinator - In a Team Swarm, the Coordinator is the Team Member who is 'in charge' of the Story being worked on. *(see Stay-At-Home, Swarmer)*

Courage - Team Members must have the courage to make reality visible, do the right thing, and work on tough problems. *(see Values)*

Cross-Functional - *(see Self-Contained)*

CURB - An acronym that stands for Complex, Unknown, Risky or Big. CURB is a mnemonic to help you remember how to determine if a functional Story is actually an Epic.

Customers - The people who will be paying for the Product, or Results, the Team is producing.

Daily Scrum - The Daily Scrum is one of the most important parts of Scrum, as it allows for a daily 'inspect and adapt' cycle. Many people misunderstand the Daily Scrum, and treat it as a simple status update. This is a mistake, as its purpose is to collect 'today's reality', compare it to the Sprint Goal and other objectives, and 'inspect and adapt' to determine what to do today. *(see Regular Sync-Up)*

Daily Standup - *(see Daily Scrum)*

Defect - 1) Anything about a Product that is seen as 'wrong' by a Stakeholder; defects usually result in a new Item being added to the Backlog; 2) A bug, failure, flaw or error in an application or program that results in unexpected, incorrect or unintended ways. *(see Bug)*

Definition of Done (DoD) - 1) The definition of Done for a Work Unit (Item, Increment, Release, ...) is the shared understanding, between the Team and the Work Unit's Stakeholders, about what it means for the Work Unit to be completed; 2) often used erroneously as a synonym for Standard of Care.

Definition of Ready (DoR) - The State a Story must be in in order to be Ready. *(see Ready Story)*

Deliverable Results - Scrum Teams produce Deliverable Results iteratively and incrementally; these Deliverable Results are often called Product. *(see Product)*

Delivery Forecast - The Delivery Forecast predicts Delivery Dates and Costs, and it should be based on Data, not Hope. It is important to note that the Team telling you they will deliver on time is not Data. Telling the Team what it will deliver, and when, is not Data.

Developer - Any member of the Scrum Team, including the people who play Product Owner and Scrum Master roles. *(synonym for Team Member)*

Development Team - The subset of the Scrum Team that is actually producing Results; this may, or may not, include the Scrum Team's Captain and Facilitator.

Do Work - Every day during the Sprint, the Team is said to "Do Work", which includes: 1) The Team Swarms with its Subject Matter Experts in order to get Stories that are 'In Progress' to "Done"; 2) As Stories get to "Done", the Team Captain determines which Ready Stories should be moved from the Work Backlog to become Work In Progress; and 3) The Team discusses and removes Impediments.

DoD - *(see Definition of Done)*

Done - A Story is Done when its Story Agreement has been met. The concept of Done has often been extended to Epics, Sprints, Releases, and so on… *(see Story Agreement) (compare to Undone)*

Done Increment - (per Ken Schwaber, Agile Project Management with Scrum, Microsoft Press, 2004, pg. 12) *"the increment consists of thoroughly tested, well-structured, and well-written code that has been built into an executable and that the user operation of the functionality is documented… This is the definition of a 'done' increment."* An Increment is Done when all the Stories involved in the Increment meet their Doneness Agreements.

Doneness Agreement - *(see Story Agreement)*

Due Diligence - A person, Team, or Organization has done its 'due diligence' when it has taken necessary steps to avoid harm to people or property.

Effort [for a Story] - The amount of time it actually took to complete a Story (meet its Agreement on Done), and is usually measured in Hours or PersonDays. *(see Story Agreement, compare to Size [of a Story])*

EffortPoint - A relative measure of the effort it will take to 'do' a Story. Often confused with StoryPoint. *(see StoryPoint, Ideal Engineering Hour/Day)*

Empirical Process - An empirical process is a process based on empiricism, which asserts that knowledge comes from experience and decisions are made based on what is known. *(synonym for agility)*

Environmental Variables - Factors affecting effort that are not related to the actual Story. These include, but are not limited to, Technical Debt, Organizational Noise, and Team Ability.

Epic - 1) an Item that is too Complex, Unknown, Risky, or Big (CURB) for the Team to agree to do all at once; 2) a named Container of other Epics and Stories. *(see CURB)*

Estimation Game - Any of a variety of consensus-based methods of estimating.

Executive Review - A Review for the business to discuss project, process, or people issues. This is not a part of Scrum, but is often necessary for legitimate business reasons. *(see Project Review, Sprint Review, Product Review, and Progress Review)*

Exemplar Story - An example Item used as a reference point for Estimation. For example, we could have exemplar Small, Medium, and Large Stories as reference points for Estimating Story Size or Effort.

Extracting Stories - The Team does Backlog Refinement with its Subject Matter Experts, its Business Owner, and its Stakeholders to assure that there are Ready Stories in the Work Backlog. This includes Extracting Stories from the Results Backlog, or Epics therein, to the Work Backlog.

eXtreme Programming (XP) - An agile development process whose practices largely focus on the production of Clean Code. *(see Clean Code)*

Feature - Something a software product enables a user to do. *(see Capability)*

Feature Complete - A state of software indicating that no more features need to be added.

Focus - Everything the Team does must have a focus, and the Team Members must focus on what is important in everything they do. *(see Values)*

Freezer - The portion of the Backlog that contains Items that are 'out of scope.'

Fridge - The portion of the Backlog that contains items that are 'in scope' but are not yet being actively Groomed for Planning. Typically, these Items are Epics or the un-decomposed remains of Epics.

Front Burner - The portion of the Backlog that the Team has agreed to work on 'now'. In Scrum this is usually called the Sprint Backlog; in Kanban this is called the Work in Progress (WIP).

Full-Time - Each Team Member belongs to a single Team. However, the Team, because it is self-organized, may 'loan out' one or more of its Team Members to work elsewhere as a Subject Matter Expert.

Functional Story - A Story that produces working code that has actual, demonstrable user value. A Functional Story's Acceptance Criteria usually consists of a single Acceptance Test, and testing to verify that the Test passes is part of the Story itself.

General Agreement - The Part of the Story Agreement that contains information about which SMEs will be involved, who will be the Story Coordinator, what is 'out of scope' for the Story, and so on. *(see Story Agreement)*

Grooming - *(see Backlog Refinement)*

Hardening Sprint - A Hardening Sprint is a specialized sprint dedicated to stabilizing the code base so that it is robust enough for release; it is often necessary because the Team failed to use an appropriate Standard of Care when it did its work. Using a Hardening Sprint is not recommended and the need for it should be addressed by improving engineering practice. If the need for hardening exists, it should be done a little at a time by using Cleanup Stories within the Sprints.

High-Ceremony Agility - Any Agile process that has many meeting, artifacts, or practices.

Humor - Everyone needs a sense of humor; if we can't laugh at some of the things we do, we'd have to cry. *(see Values)*

Hybridized Agile - An approach to create a better breed of agile by combining various agile and existing processes; this often leads to paradigm induced blindness. *(see paradigm induced blindness)*

Ideal Effort - The amount of effort it would take to build something if conditions were as they should be; there are no impediments of any kind, and you don't require any magic or miracles. *(see Ideal Engineering Hour/ Day)*

Ideal Engineering Hour/Day - An estimate of effort that assumes no disruptions or disasters; an Ideal Hour/Day is an Hour/Day that has no interruptions. *(see Ideal Effort)*

Impediment - Anything that is causing the Team to not be at its best. These could be fears, risks, or problems.

InBox - Items in the Backlog that have not yet been prioritized.

Increment - As the Team completes each Story, it continuously produces Results (proposed and partial Deliverables) that require Stakeholder feedback. This continuous collection of accumulated Results is called the Increment; the increment should always be "Done" and in reviewable condition.

Informed Process - An informed process is one in which decision-making is informed by gathering observations in progressive steps. *(synonym for Agile Process)*

Interested Bystander - People who think that they are Stakeholders, but actually 'don't matter' to you, are called Interested Bystanders.

Intraspective - A discussion by the Scrum Team about its Practices or Teamwork that occurs *within* the Sprint: it is often precipitated by an event that 'didn't go well.' *(compare to Retrospective)*

Intrinsic Difficulty - The Intrinsic Difficulty of a Functional Story is inherent in the Acceptance Criteria, and is based on the complexity involved in the design activities themselves and the complexity of the resulting designs and algorithms. *(see Size [of a Story])*

Item - A single unit of work on the Backlog, an Item is either an Epic or a Story.

Kanban Method - 1) A method of organizing and managing the work for delivering services to customers. The main strength of Kanban (from a Scrum point of view) is that its Planning is continuous, which makes it more likely to keep up with reality, and hence more agile.

Kanban Values - The Kanban Values are: Respect, Values, Focus, transparency, Understanding, Leadership, Agreement, Collaboration, and Flow. *(see Values)*

Kanban(ish) Variant - The Kanban(ish) Variant of Scrum is one in which the standard (batch) Sprint Planning is replaced by continuous Planning throughout the Sprint. When doing the Kanban(ish) variant of Scrum, the Sprint Planning session 1) determines when the Sprint will end, 2) selects enough Stories to start work, 3) chooses a Kaizen to work on in the next Sprint, and 4) creates its Sprint Goal.

Kaizen - 1) A philosophy of continuous improvement of working practices, personal efficiency, etc, and 2) a single improvement for a person, Team, or Organization.

Leadership - 1) The act of being followed, 2) The interplay between decision-making and team direction. *(see Values)*

Leadership Team - A Scrum Team that consists of Team Captains (Product Owners) from different Teams along with its own Team Captain and Scrum Master. The purpose of the Leadership Team is to coordinate cross-cutting issues, foster communications, and enable collaboration across the Teams. In particular, the Leadership Team is accountable for dividing the work up among their Scrum Teams. *(also called Product Owner Team, Management Team)*

Lean Principles - Lean Principles focus on creating value while eliminating waste, thus making a Value Stream (process flow) more efficient. Two of the Lean Principles that are built into *good* implementations of Scrum are 'Pull, don't Push' and 'Minimize Inventory.'

Mental Agility - Having situational awareness and using feedback to make the decisions necessary to be agile. *(see agility, Physical Agility)*

Mission - A short statement of why the Team exists – what it does, for whom, and why – the Mission is often obvious from looking at the Team's name.

MTS - Stands for Multi-Team Scrum and is a description of Scrum found in the *Scrum Handbook: Multi-Team Scrum.*

One Big Thing (OBT) - In any model, any entity in the model should be defined by 'One Big Thing'; its reason for being. If you can't find the One Big Thing for any given entity, then either the model is defective, or you don't understand the model.

Openness - There should be no secrets between/amongst Team Members about things relevant to the work and their ability to do the work. *(see Values)*

Order - Refers to the order of the Backlog; the order that the Product Owner wants the Items worked on. *(see Priority)*

Organizational Noise - An Organization that empowers and nurtures its Teams is said to be a 'quiet' Organization, while one with many procedures, meetings, interruptions, and the like, is said to be 'noisy.' *(see Environmental Variables)*

Pairing - Pairing, a practice often associated with eXtreme Programming (XP), is when each Story is worked on by two Developers, working side-by-side at one computer, collaborating on the same design, algorithm, code or test. Many Teams have found it useful to rotate Pairs every 1-2 hours, which is referred to as Polygamous Pairing.

Paradigm Induced Blindness - When a person follows a process 'blindly' because the process is so convoluted it just overloads a person's head.

Physical Agility - A Team, Project, or Organization has Physical Agility if its processes provide opportunities to obtain the feedback necessary to enable agility. *(see agility, Mental Agility)*

PlaceHolder Story - A PlaceHolder Story is a Story that represents a 'known unknown' (or contains StoryPoints to be used for 'known unknowns'). One of the most common issues for Scrum Teams is what to do about work that it expects to have to do during a Sprint, but doesn't actually know the details about yet, such as fixing bugs in existing systems, or expected sales support efforts. Using PlaceHolder Stories is a form of buffer and is used as part of contingency planning.

Plan of Action - A tentative plan, developed by the Team, of how the Sprint might be carried out. The purpose of the Plan of Action is not to have a plan, per se, but to enable the Team to justify to itself that doing the work is possible. *(see Sprint Planning)*

Planning - A session with the whole Scrum Team (including the Team Captain/Product Owner) to decide which Stories should be "Done" next. *(see Sprint Planning)*

Planning Day - Planning day takes place 'between' Sprints, and includes the Sprint Review (broken into the Product and Progress Reviews when necessary), the Retrospective, and Sprint Planning for the next Sprint.

Potentially Releasable Increment - *(see Done Increment)*

Potentially Shippable Increment - *(see Done Increment)*

Priority - The priority of an Item is based on how important it is. Normally, the importance of an Item would be based on its Business Value, but in Scrum, an Item's priority is determined by when it will be done, not by how valuable it is. *(see Order)*

Product - 1) (in Scrum) Whatever the Team produces; the Team's Work Results; 2) (in popular use) A particular marketable/sellable/usable unit, such as 'website ABC' or the '123 Counting Program.'

Product Backlog - *(see Backlog)*

Product Backlog Item - *(see Item)*

Product Champion - A type of Business Owner whose Results Backlog represents a single Product. The Product Champion owns the Product Vision, represents this Product's Clients and Customers to the Organization, and provides/identifies subject matter expertise to the Organization to aid in development and reviews.

Product Increment - *(see Increment)*

Production - The act of actually producing Results. *(see Development Team)*

Product Owner - The Scrum Team Member who is accountable to the Business for both the value of the Team's Work, and the value of the Team's Results. This role is often confused with the non-Scrum role of Product Manager, who is accountable to the Business for the Product. *(see Product Ownership)*

Product Owner Team - *(see Leadership Team)*

Product Ownership - The collection of Responsibilities and Accountabilities that sit between the Stakeholders and the Developers; these responsibilities range from creating a strategic vision to delivery management to determining what work will be done next. *(see Team Captain, Business Owner, Agile Actuary)*

Product Review - A Team session at the end of a Sprint where the Team (along with its Business Owner and Team Captain) reviews their Work Results with Stakeholders in order to get feedback on what to do next, what to do better, and so on. *(see Sprint Review, Progress Review)*

Product Vision - The product vision statement is a quick summary expressing how the product supports the Organization and/or Stakeholders.

Progress Review - A meeting with the Team Captain, Agile Actuary, Business Owner, and Customers about 'how the work is going' — information to help update the Delivery Forecast and set expectations with the Customers. *(See Executive Review, Sprint Review, Product Review)*

Project Review - *(See Progress Review)*

'Pull' Feedback - Feedback obtained by actively engaging a stakeholder during review of any product artifact (completed story or product increment). *(see 'Catch' Feedback)*

Quality Code - *(see Clean Code)*

Ready - *(see Definition of Ready)*

Ready Story - A Story that is small, well-defined and ready to take to Planning. Generally, this means that the Story's Agreement is a '10 minute discussion' away from being agreed to. *(see Well-Defined Story)*

Refactoring - Rewriting existing source code in order to improve its readability, reusability or structure without affecting its meaning or behavior.

Refinement - *(see Backlog Refinement)*

Regular Sync-Up - A re-plan/plan the Team has on a regular basis (typically daily) in order to collect together an understanding of 'changes in reality' in order to deal with it. *(see Daily Scrum)*

Regulators - Entities, either inside or outside your Business Organization, who can regulate, or constrain, the Product/Results the Team is producing and/or the process that the Team uses. Examples include things like Cyber Security, CISA, ITAR Compliance, SOX, Medical, etc.

Regulatory Constraint - An official standard, rule, or regulation that can effect either what is built (e.g., it must be bi-lingual), how it is built (e.g., the Code must be completely protected by Tests), or both. *(see Regulators)*

Release - A movement of the Team's Product from the development environment to some other environment, for some other reason than development. Examples include alpha releases, beta releases, go-live releases, releases to a test lab, and so on. Actually Releasing something is not a part of Scrum; releasing product must be done through Stories – there is no 'release' ceremony in Scrum.

Release Sprint - A specialized Sprint whose purpose is to Release Product; it contains Stories specific to Release Activities and finishing Undone Work. A Release Sprint usually contains no additional development. *(see Undone)*

Release Strategy - A term used to refer to all types of Release Planning, Release Monitoring, and the like. It is not a part of Scrum, but a Release Strategy is often needed with Scrum – in part to decide what work will be left UnDone until the Release Sprint.

Respect - Respect is the belief that people are always doing the best they can do at any given moment. *(see Values)*

Responsible - Responsible people are the individual(s) who actually do the work; responsibility can be shared. The degree of responsibility is determined by the person with the "Accountability"; and Responsibility is often confused with Accountability. *(see Accountable)*

Results - *(see Work Results)*

Results Backlog - A prioritized list of Results (Deliverables) that the Business Owner hopes to deliver to the Stakeholders. The Stakeholders and Business Owner maintain the Results Backlog, by adding new Deliverables to the Results Backlog, and prioritizing/re-prioritizing the Results Backlog. *(see Business Owner)*

Retrospective - *(see Team Retrospective)*

Review - *(see Sprint Review)*

Rhythm - Movement or procedure with uniform or patterned recurrence. Scrum has two primary Rhythms: the Daily rhythm of work, and the Sprintly rhythm of feedback and planning. Also referred to as Cadence.

Scale-Ready - A single-team process or practice is said to be 'scale-ready' when it can be easily applied or extended to an organization of many teams.

Scaling - The changes in Structure and Governance that enable successful growth (or reduction) of production. In general, the increase or decrease in one or more dimensions of an organization in order to improve success.

Scenario - An interaction with the System that consists of a single thread, and is represented by a single Acceptance Test. *(see Use Case)*

Scrum - An agile framework (or process) for Product Development, not Project Management. There have been, are, and will be, may variants of Scrum; it is more of a concept than a prescription.

Scrum$_P$ - Scrum$_P$ is a variant of Scrum in which the Product Owner 'lives with' the Stakeholders and is their representative to the Team. In Scrum$_P$ the Product Owner may not change priorities during the Sprint.

Scrum$_G$ - Scrum$_G$ is a variant of Scrum in which the Product Owner is a member of the Team who consults with the Stakeholders. In Scrum$_G$ the Team's Product Owner may work with the Team to change priorities during the Sprint.

Scrum$_H$ - Scrum$_H$ is a variant of Scrum in which Product Ownership is shared between a Team Captain on the Team and a Business Owner outside the Team. In Scrum$_H$ the Team's Team Captain may work with the Team to change priorities during the Sprint.

Scrum-of-Scrums (SoS) - In a multi-scrum-team environment:

1) a meeting held after all the individual Scrum Teams' Daily Scrums, consisting of a representative from each Scrum Team, in order to achieve cross-team collaboration; 2) a virtual Scrum Team composed of the Scrum Masters from each Scrum Team; and 3) any virtual Scrum Team composed of representatives from various Scrum Teams.

Scrum Board - *(see Story Board)*

Scrum Master - *(see Team Facilitator)*

Scrum Master Community - The collection of people doing Scrum Mastering within an Organization; this includes Team Facilitators. Agile Coaches, and Change Agents. This group is responsible for 'making Scrum better' within the Organization. They have a Backlog (often virtual or invisible) of changes they would like to have in the Organization to make it more amenable to Scrum.

Scrum Mastering - Enabling and Empowering People, Teams, and Organizations in order to allow them to do their jobs better. People playing Scrum Master roles apply Servant Leadership principles to teamwork and practices in order to make them more effective and enjoyable. *(see Team Facilitator, Agile Coach, Change Agent)*

Scrum Team - A Scrum Team (commonly called the "Team") is a small, co-located, self-organized, self-contained, value-driven, group of full-time Team Members who are organized around a Mission. Their job is to produce high Quality Results at a Sustainable Pace. Two of the Team Members have special accountabilities: the Team Captain (Product Owner) and the Team Facilitator (Scrum Master).

Scrum Values - The Scrum Values are: Openness, Focus, Respect Commitment, and Courage. *(see Values)*

Self-Contained - A self-contained (also called cross-functional) team is one that contains all the knowledge and skills necessary to accomplish its objectives and goals: in software development this means that there are people who can test, there are people who can code, there are people who do analysis, there are people who write documentation, and so on.

Self-Organized - A self-organized team is one that chooses how best to accomplish its work, rather than being directed (micro-managed) by others outside the team. *(see Tactical Agility)*

Single Item Flow - Single item flow (also called 'single piece flow' or 'one piece flow') is a lean manufacturing concept that says that each individual Item will move through the manufacturing process *all at once* with no waiting between steps. On Scrum Teams, this means Stories don't wait for people who have skills they need – the people are available when they're needed. *(see Team Swarm)*

Size [of a Story] - The Size of a Functional Story is a measure of the Story's Intrinsic Difficulty. (see *Intrinsic Difficulty, Story Size, compare to Effort [for a Story]*)

SME - *(see Subject Matter Expert)*

SME Availability - This is an Environmental Variable that indicates whether or not there are Subject Matter Experts available who have the knowledge or expertise you need, when you need it. *(see Environmental Variables)*

SoC - *(see Standard of Care)*

Spike - An XP (eXtreme Programming) term that describes Stories that figure out answers to tough technical or design problems. Spikes address only the problem under consideration and ignore all other concerns. Most Spikes get thrown away, which differentiates them from Architecturally Significant Stories.

Sprint - A fixed period of time (less than a month) during which a Team produces Work Results for review. The Sprint length is defined by the interval between Product Reviews, is usually consistent across Sprints, and must not be changed once the Sprint has started.

Sprint Backlog - The Stories the Team has (currently) selected to work on during the Sprint. This includes their Agreements and (possibly) Tasks. *(see Front Burner, Sprint Forecast)*

Sprint Cancellation - *(see Cancelling a Sprint)*

Sprint Commitment - The Team commits to its Sprint Goal and to doing due diligence in order to have all completed Stories meet their Agreements. The Team does *not* commit to doing all the Stories in the Sprint Backlog.

Sprint End - The time when work in the Sprint is interrupted in order to Review, Retrospect, and Plan. The Sprint End is usually a set date and time, but may be pre-determined by an event, as "We'll have Sprint End and do the Reviews when Doug gets back from Europe..."

Sprint Forecast - The Team's best guess about how many Items will fit into the next Sprint. The Sprint Backlog is, at most, a forecast: not a plan, commitment, or promise.

Sprint Goal - The Sprint Goal is a single, clear, benefit that defines success for the Sprint. According to the Scrum Guide, "The Sprint Goal is an objective that *will be met* within the Sprint..." – it is a commitment, not an aspiration.

Sprint Interrupt - At the end of the Sprint the Team interrupts the continuous flow of work and has four Ceremonies/Discussions/ Meetings in order to allow for Feedback, Improvement, and Re-Planning. *(see Sprint Planning, Team Retrospective, Product Review, Progress Review)*

Sprint Planning - A Team session at the beginning of a Sprint in which the Team Members (including the Team Captain) discuss and negotiate amongst themselves in order to: 1) Establish Sprint End; 2) Select a Kaizen to accomplish; 3) Make sure there are enough Stories Ready or 'in progress' so the Team can get back to work; and 4) Commit to a Sprint Goal.

Sprint Retrospective - *(see Team Retrospective)*

Sprint Review - The Sprint Review is supposed to be a Product Review, but many Teams include other reviews, as well... this is usually *not* a good thing. *(see Executive Review, Project Review, and Product Review)*

Sprint Team - The Scrum Team *along* with any external SMEs who are (either officially or unofficially) members of the Team during the Sprint.

Sprint Zero - A deprecated synonym for Startup Sprint.

Stakeholder - 1) A person with a *legitimate* interest in the Product, Process, or Team. 2) Someone who the Scrum Team ignores 'at their peril.' 3) A person who reviews the Team's Work Results at the Product Review. *Note: while Team Members are stakeholders, the word Stakeholder [uppercase] is usually reserved for external stakeholders.*

Standard of Care (SoC) - The Standard of Care is a portion of the Story's Agreement, and is the description of the objective criteria the Team will use to determine whether or not a Story meets internal standards or constraints, as opposed to providing external Stakeholder Value. The Standard of Care is used to 'guarantee' sufficient technical quality to be releasable. Failure to meet the Standard of Care is negligence, and the Team is accountable for any damages that result. *(see Story Agreement)*

Startup Sprint - A specialized Sprint used to get a Team 'up and running' quickly, rather than dragging their feet *getting ready* to start development. A Startup Sprint usually includes Analysis, Team Training, Infrastructure and Environmental Work – and the development of something 'real' – and its purpose is to limit the amount of 'up front' work that takes place before actual Product is developed. It is a Sprint whose Sprint Goal is "We will be producing real Results by the end of this Sprint" - it is not about 'getting ready' it is about 'getting moving'.

Stay-At-Home - In swarming, a person who 'stays with' the Story, and probably works as the Story's Coordinator. When working on Coding Stories, it is common to have a Coder as the Stay-At-Home in order to avoid context-switching.

Story - 1) A request from a Stakeholder for something of value. 2) A unit of work that is 'small enough' to be agreed to by the Team; an Item that is not an Epic. 3) (by others) A synonym for Backlog Item. 3) (by others) a synonym for User Story.

Story Agreement - An agreement between the Product Owner and the rest of the Team that defines when a Story will be complete (or Done). The Story Agreement consists of the Acceptance Criteria, the Standard of Care, and possibly additional General Agreements. When all of the Story Agreements are met this can be accepteted as the Definition of Done or simply called "Done". This notion can be extended to Capabilities, Sprints, Releases, and so on… this is a synonym for "Done."

Story Board - A Team tool that shows the tasks that are needed in the Sprint, organized by Story. The Scrum Board is a 'living' document that the Team updates to reflect its current thinking; this is often done at the Daily Scrum.

Story Owner - A Team Member (or SME) who represents the Stakeholder's interests in the Story to the rest of the Team during Planning and Development.

Story Size - A measure of how much product will be produced by the Story. *(see Size [of a Story])*

Story Time - *(see Backlog Refinement)*

Storyotype - A storyotype or template for a Story or Epic. Storyotypes are used to capture re-useful information common to many Stories; in particular, Storyotypes are used to capture common Standards of Care.

StoryPoint - A relative measure of the size of a Story. Often confused with EffortPoint. *(see EffortPoint, Velocity)*

Strategic Agility - Agility that changes 'what' the Team or Organization does in order to maximize Value or ROI. Strategic Agility is a Product Ownership responsibility. *(compare to Tactical Agility)*

STS - Stands for Single-Team Scrum and is a description Scrum found in the *Scrum HandBook: Single-Team Scrum.*

Subject Matter Expert (SME) - Somebody with specialized knowledge or talent that is needed by the Team; this includes SMEs on the product, the environment, development practices, and so on. The term usually refers to SMEs that are 'outside' the Team, but not always.

Sustainable Pace - The rate at which a Team can work without burning itself out. Originally called "40 Hour Week" by Kent Beck as an XP practice.

Swarm - *(see Team Swarm)*

Swarmer - In a Team Swarm, a Swarmer is a person who is moving from Story to Story, working with those Story's Coordinators and other Swarmers, in order to offer his or her expertise and efforts wherever they are needed.

Swarming - Having several people work together on a piece of work. Common swarming patterns in software development include: Pair Programming, Three People at a Whiteboard, and Team at a Table. *(see Team Swarm)*

Tactical Agility - Agility that changes 'how' a Team works in order to get to Done; this is embodied in the Team's Self-Organization. *(compare to Strategic Agility)*

Task - A small, undivided, 'chunk' of work to be done or undertaken, usually within the Team. Tasks compose the team's internal plan on how they will get Stories to Done.

Team - 1) The Scrum Team; 2) (by others) The Development Team; 3) (Ken Schwaber) A role, taken on by a group of people, that means that they are a Well-Formed Team.

Team Ability - Team Ability includes the capabilities of individual Team Members, the Team's frame of mind, and how well the Team synergizes. *(see Environmental Variables)*

Team Captain - The Team Member who is accountable to the Business (usually represented by a single Business Owner) for maximizing the value of the Team's Work. Each Team must have its own Team Captain to 'call the plays' about what work the Team should do next. *(see Product Ownership)*

Team Facilitator - The Team Member who is accountable for making sure that Scrum is used correctly, that the Team uses Scrum in a positive way, and that the Team is constantly improving its use of Scrum. *(see Scrum Mastering)*

Team Member - Any member of the Scrum Team, including the Team Captain (Product Owner) and Team Facilitator (Scrum Master).

Team Retrospective - A Team session at the end of a Sprint when the Team Members (facilitated by their Team Facilitator with, possibly, support from an Agile Coach) discuss and agree upon ways they could improve their Practices, teamwork, environment, or Organization for the next Sprint.

Team Swarm - A method of working where a Team works on just a few Stories at a time. Each Story is finished as quickly as possible by having many people work on it together, rather than having a series of handoffs. The ultimate in Swarming is Single Item Flow, where the Team works on *only* one Story at a time, and finishes it completely before moving on to the next one.

Team Values - The Team Values are: Openness, Focus, Respect, Commitment, Courage, Visibility, Humor, and Accountability. *(see Values, Scrum Values, Kanban Values)*

TeamLet - The Team Members and SMEs who are Swarming on a particular Story. The typical swarm involves 2-3 people at a time. *(see Team Swarm)*

Technical Debt - Deficiencies in the code, technical documentation, development environments, 3rd-party tools, and development practices, which makes it hard for the Team to modify, update, repair, or deliver the Product. *(see Environmental Variables)*

Time-Boxed Story - Time-Boxed Stories have their Doneness defined by a time-box, and the actual Results produced are limited to what can be completed in that time-box. *(see Acceptance-Based Story)*

UnDone - The phrase "UnDone work" is often used to describe the work needed to move something from Done to Releasable; in other words, it is work that *maybe should have been* done, but wasn't. Deciding what work to leave Undone is a delicate issue. *(see Done)*

Use Case - A Capability that represents an interaction between a User and the System in order to achieve a Goal. A Use Case consists of multiple Scenarios, and usually requires many Stories to implement, so a Use Case is usually an Epic. *(see Scenario)*

User Story - A Story whose value is for the User of the software; popularized by eXtreme Programming (XP).

Validation - Validation is assuring that a Result (Capability) is fit for use; that it does what it *needs* to do. *(compare to Verification)*

Value-Driven - A Team is value-driven when the Team Members value working together; they are constantly improving themselves, their Team, their environment, and their tools; and they strive to live an appropriate set of Values. *(see Values)*

Values - The word Values, in common use, refers either to values in general, the Team Values, the Kanban Values, the Scrum Values, or any other list of Values. *(see Team Values, Kanban Values, Scrum Values)*

Velocity - The rate that a Team or Organization *has been producing* Product; usually calculated as completed StoryPoints per Sprint. It is often used as an approximation for Capacity and is often confused with WorkRate. *(see StoryPoint, Capacity, WorkRate)*

Verification - Verification is assuring that something has met its specification; that it does as it was *intended* to do. *(compare to Validation)*

Visibility - The Team makes the current state of the Team's Product/Results visible to Stakeholders and the Business. *(see Values)*

Walking Skeleton - A subset of the System that demonstrates the basic architectural decisions; it is the result of many Architecturally Significant Stories.

Well-Defined Story - A Story whose Acceptance Criteria are known. *(compare to Ready Story)*

Well-Formed Team (WFT) - A Well-Formed Team (WFT) is more than just a Team; it's a 'real Team' – a Team that knows its job, does its job, and looks good doing it. A WFT is a Team with heart and soul; where Team Members value working together to be the best Team they can be. A WFT is a team that is self-organized, self-contained, and value-driven. A Scrum Team is a well-formed team that has both a Product Owner and a Scrum Master (Team Captain and Facilitator), and it is a primary teaching of Scrum that all teams (especially those working in complex domains) should be well-formed.

Whole Team - The Scrum Team along with its Subject Matter Experts and its Stakeholders; this is the 'whole team' involved in production.

WIBNI (wib'•nee) - stands for **W**ouldn't **I**t **B**e **N**ice **I**f, and represents things that we wish were true, but aren't – so we must get over them; example is "wouldn't it be nice if we had more testers…"

WIP - *(see Work in Progress)*

WIP Limit - The maximum number of Stories allowed in the Work in Progress at any given time. *(see Work in Progress)*

Work Backlog - The Team's Work Backlog is owned by the Team Captain and consists of the Stories that the Team expects to be asked to work on 'soon'. These Stories are of two types: Capabilities and Chores. *(see Capability, Chore)*

Work in Progress (WIP) - The Stories that the Team is currently working on. *(see Front Burner)*

Work Item - The Work Items the Scrum Team works on are called Stories, and as the Team completes the Stories, they produce Results in an iterative and incremental manner, thus providing opportunities for meaningful feedback from Stakeholders.

WFT - *(see Well-Formed Team)*

WorkRate - The rate that a Team works; usually calculated as EffortPoints per Sprint, Ideal Engineering Hours/Days per Sprint, or something similar. It is used as an aid in Sprint Planning, and is often confused with Velocity. *(see EffortPoints, Ideal Engineering Hours/Days, Velocity)*

Work Results - Whatever an individual or Team produces. *(see Product)*

XP - *(see eXtreme Programming)*

SECTION 4

Appendix

Nine Zones of Scrum

A Taxonomy of Scrums

		Locked Down Sprint	Adaptable Sprint	Continuous Planning
>> Collaboration >>	Two Product Owners	Scrum 2.5	Scrum 2.75	Scrum 3.0
	Tactical Product Owner	Scrum 1.75	Scrum 2.0	Scrum 2.25
	Strategic Product Owner	Scrum 1.0	Scrum 1.25	Scrum 1.5
		>> *Responsiveness* >>		

3 Recursive Steps for Improvement

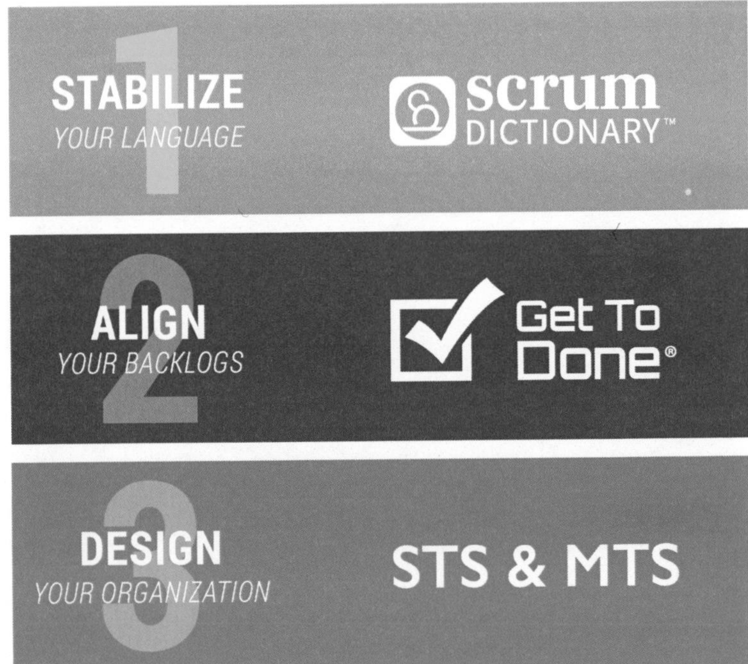

SECTION 5

Acknowledgements

We have been involved in Scrum for over 20 years, and we'd like to thank Ken Schwaber and Jeff Sutherland for bringing Scrum to the software community. Without them, there would be no Scrum.

We would also like to thank all the teams we have worked with and observed, and all our students who have brought us news and information about their Scrum teams. We know that *"Scrum is what successful Scrum Teams do,"* and without this feedback about what successful Scrum Teams do, there would be no Scrum$_H$.

Good luck, and happy scrumming!

About the Authors

Dan Rawsthorne

Dan has developed software in an agile way since 1983. He has worked in many different domains, from e-commerce to military avionics. He has a PhD in Mathematics (number theory), is a retired Army Officer, and a Professional Bowler and Coach. Dan is very active in the Agile/Scrum community and speaks quite often at conferences and seminars. He is a transformation agent, coaching Organizations to become more successful through agility. His non-software background has helped him immeasurably in his coaching: his formal training in mathematics guides him to look for underlying problems rather than focus on surface symptoms; his military background helps him understand the importance of teamwork and empowerment; and his work with bowlers has helped him understand that coaching is a two-way street.

Doug Shimp

Doug has worked in the technology field since 1992 and has played many key roles on software teams, including Coder, Tester, Analyst, Team Leader, Manager, Coach, and Consultant. Doug's passion is for team learning to improve product development, and he is a leader in the area of Agile/Scrum transitions and applied practices. He believes that the core basis for applied agility is that 'You must see the result for it to be real; otherwise it is all just theory...' Much of his experience with teamwork and agility comes from outside the software field, including an earlier career as an owner/manager of a painting company – which enabled him to learn about small-team dynamics in a very hands-on way.

For More Information

To learn more about 3Back, LLC and our Scrum related services, contact us at info@3back.com. Follow @Scrum_Coach on Twitter, and to subscribe to our newsletter, visit: https://blog.3back.com/.

We Make Teams Better

We don't just talk Agile, we live Agile. Our 3Back Team is a well-formed, Agile team; applying Scrum_H in our own workplace. From our hands-on support staff to our seasoned consultants and trainers, every member of the 3Back Team is, at minimum, a CSM (Certified Scrum Master). Within every level of the 3Back team, we bring a real world appreciation and understanding of your team's needs.

Managing work

At 3Back we are a fully distributed team. We actively build and manage Get To Done (gettodone.com), an online Scrum software development tool. Get To Done helps us train as a pedagogical tool, explore new ways of collaborating and focus our most precious resource, attention, on work being done.

14550315R00074

Made in the USA
Lexington, KY
08 November 2018